AF669610

Whispers of the Zen Forest

Master Mindfulness, Meditation, and Positive Thinking with Short Zen Stories to Relieve Stress, Overcome Anxiety, and Achieve Inner Peace

By

Sati Siroda

Book Ecke

Whispers of the Zen Forest

Master Mindfulness, Meditation, and Positive Thinking with Short Zen Stories to Relieve Stress, Overcome Anxiety, and Achieve Inner Peace

By

Sati Siroda

Published by Book Ecke
15A, 4th Floor, City Vista, Tower A,
Suite No.1140, Fountain Road, Kharadi, Pune - 411014
Website: www.bookecke.com

© Copyright Sati Siroda, 2025 - All rights reserved.

The content contained within this book may not be reproduced, duplicated or transmitted without direct written permission from the author or the publisher.

Under no circumstances will any blame or legal responsibility be held against the publisher or author for any damages, reparation, or monetary loss due to the information contained within this book. Either directly or indirectly. You are responsible for your own choices, actions, and results.

Legal Notice:

This book is copyright-protected. This book is only for personal use. You cannot amend, distribute, sell, use, quote or paraphrase any part or the content within this book without the consent of the author or publisher.

Disclaimer Notice:

Please note the information contained within this document is for educational and entertainment purposes only. All effort has been executed to present accurate, up-to-date, and reliable, complete information. No warranties of any kind are declared or implied. Readers acknowledge that the author is not engaging in the rendering of legal, financial, medical or professional advice. The content within this book has been derived from various sources. Please consult a licensed professional before attempting any techniques outlined in this book. Fair use of AI tools has been employed selectively to enhance the creation of this book.

By reading this document, the reader agrees that under no circumstances is the author responsible for any losses, direct or indirect, which are incurred as a result of the use of the information contained within this document, including, but not limited to, — errors, omissions, or inaccuracies.

For permission requests, contact **support@bookecke.com.**

ISBN

eBook: 978-81-986117-2-7

Paperback: 978-81-986117-0-3

Hardback: 978-81-986117-7-2

First edition [2025]

Cover Art: Safeer Ahmed

Visit www.bookecke.com for any further information.

To Life, my greatest guide—

For every whisper of joy, silence, sorrow, and awakening.

And to those who lit the path with presence,

Your wisdom lives gently within me.

…and to Asoka Siroda—

Thank you for walking this winding path beside me,

For every quiet step,

For every unspoken promise

That we would find our way, together.

BOOKS BY SATI SIRODA

Mind the Quote

Poulomi's Abode of Thoughts

Coffee Tales: Short Stories of Wisdom

Earnest Poetica: Ink Expressions of the Ineffable Heart

Gratitude Journal: Reflect, Appreciate, Transform in 60 Days

Inspiring Stories for Amazing Girls Who Believe in Themselves

Inspiring Stories for Amazing Boys Who Believe in Themselves

I Am 6 and Wonderful

I Am 6 and Brave

Table of Contents

Foreword

Indeed, amid life's chaos, finding inner peace and tranquility can seem like an insurmountable task. Yet, the timeless wisdom of the *Pali Canon* offers a guiding light on this journey. In *"Whispers of the Zen Forest," Sati Siroda* skillfully weaves together ancient teachings with modern storytelling, creating a distinctive and accessible guide for navigating the complexities of the human experience. It is a sincere and contemplative work that invites the reader to pause, breathe, and return to the simplicity of mindful living.

Through the lens of mindfulness, meditation, and positive thinking, this book provides a powerful framework for overcoming anxiety, stress, and uncertainty. By embracing the principles outlined in these pages, readers can cultivate a more profound sense of inner peace, clarity, and purpose.

Drawing on years spent walking beside and guiding others on the path of mindful living, I have witnessed the profound power of the Buddha's teachings to restore balance, compassion, and resilience in people's lives. At the Sanghakaya Foundation, where I am fortunate to serve, we are dedicated to supporting individuals on their journey to awakening. We believe that the eternal insights of the Buddha remain as relevant today as it was centuries ago, offering the key to true happiness and lasting fulfillment.

I am delighted to recommend *Whispers of the Zen Forest* to anyone seeking a more mindful, compassionate, and meaningful life. May the wisdom contained within these pages continue to guide you on your journey and inspire a quiet strength within. May you discover peace, love, and liberation in the whispers of the Zen forest.

With blessings of peace and metta,

Ajahn Prashil Ratana Gautam

Advisor, World Alliance of Buddhists (WAB)

Head Monk, Sanghakaya Foundation [45]

Author's Note

A Whisper That Changed Everything

I was 10 years old when I first encountered the way of the Buddha—not in a book, but by standing in awe in the hills of Dharamshala, India, just outside the monastery of His Holiness the Dalai Lama. I remember being captivated not by the monastery itself, but by a young monk walking silently with such stillness that I didn't want to leave. Something in me recognized a life I didn't yet understand but deeply longed for. I told my mother, with all the innocence in the world, that I wanted to stay back and become a renunciate.

Coming from a different belief system, my mother lovingly distracted me with a promise of buying a Tibetan dress. Though I was young and easily persuaded, the seed had already been planted. That moment left a quiet, lasting imprint. Over time, I became deeply curious about Buddhist philosophy and the way practitioners lived—with simplicity, restraint, and peace. I explored many traditions—Theravāda, Zen, Chan—and I longed to undertake Vipassana. But as life often does, it led me elsewhere.

Then came 2020—and with it, a stillness that changed everything.

One ordinary April afternoon, while I was busy saving a tiny kitten, a mosquito quietly found its way to me. I was soon diagnosed with severe dengue. Hospitals, overwhelmed and collapsing under the weight of the pandemic, had no space for anyone but COVID patients. Doors were closed, and hope seemed like a luxury. No beds, no proper medication, no admission. My condition deteriorated quickly. Days passed as I lay at home, burning with an unrelenting fever, my platelets plummeting with every hour.

One night, when my body burned beyond measure and my vomiting turned bloodied, my little cocker spaniel, Oscar, grew visibly alarmed—whimpering, pacing, sensing something was terribly wrong. Asoka rushed to me, lifted me into his arms, and carried me to the nearest hospital. While he stood at the hospital reception pleading for admission, our doctor—still at home and just preparing to leave—spoke with the staff and higher authorities over the phone, urging them to admit me. My condition had worsened to the point that they could no longer hesitate.

And then came the moment I can never forget. I lay there—weak, fading, barely conscious—when I overheard a familiar voice again, calm but urgent:

"I'll be there soon... but I think she only has fifteen minutes."

In that moment, time collapsed. My entire life—the chasing, the proving, the accumulating—fell away. I was simply a breath away from the unknown, lying under bright hospital lights, while Asoka stood at the ward's door—watching, praying, silently pleading with life itself. I saw the fear in his eyes, and in that silence, a promise forming between us:

"If there's another chance... we will do it right."

When I woke up the next morning, still alive, it took a moment to understand what had happened. Asoka was still watching me—eyes tired, but steady. We had both been given something sacred: a second chance. My recovery was slow, and my hopes were fragile. Some days felt like borrowed time, and my weakness gave way to despair—recovery felt nearly impossible.

From that point forward, I began studying the teachings with sincerity—not as philosophy, but as breath, as ground beneath me. I completed an online introductory course on Buddhist wisdom through HarvardX, offered by Harvard University, and studied with renewed intention, marking the beginning of a transformation in my way of life. Even in my weakened physical state, I committed wholly to the path—offering what strength I had, one breath at a time.

One night, when it still felt like I might not survive, Asoka asked, *"What's your last wish?"*

I whispered, "Take me to any monastery. If they won't allow me in because of COVID, let me stay just outside. I just want to be close to peace."

Without hesitation, he said, "Then I will be with you."

The second lockdown began before we could go. So instead, we turned inward. Later, we shared an extravagant meal as our final meal before starting our journey anew. It was a humble goodbye to our old lifestyle. The next day onward, we changed our food and lifestyle, and we embraced the five precepts, beginning to practice earnestly. We eventually undertook Vipassana training and continued learning from monks across different traditions and countries. In April 2022, we formally received our precepts and offered our hearts, without reservation, to the path.

Though we had practiced meditation for over twenty years before that, it was only then that we began to truly *live* it. To understand it not as a technique, but as surrender, as presence, as peace.

The path did not create any magic and take suffering away from my life—it transformed how I walked through it.

It gave me the wisdom to hold pain with compassion. It gave me clarity, direction, and a quiet joy I had never known before.

This book is an offering from that journey. Each part is a reflection of a whisper I once heard in the stillness—whispers that led me gently, unwaveringly, home.

With deep gratitude,

Sati

Introduction

Dear Seeker of Stillness,

Before anything else, let me gently remind you:

You already carry within you the peace you seek.

It may have been buried beneath the noise of daily life, the distractions of thought, or the weight of past and future. But it is there—quiet, unwavering, waiting for you to return.

This book, *Whispers of the Zen Forest*, is an invitation to return.

Within these pages *are 50 short, reflective stories* written in a *Zen-inspired style*. This book also offers:

- *Bite-sized teachings* that fit easily into your daily life
- *Short meditations* after every part to help you practice, not just read

These are original, modern expressions shaped by quiet wisdom and woven with timeless insights. Each chapter draws from *a quote of the Buddha,* carefully chosen from the *Pali Canon* [52] *as it is*—the earliest complete collection of the Buddha's teachings. After each story, you'll find:

- A *contemplative reflection,* designed to speak directly to the heart
- A *real-life application example*, helping you embody the teaching in your daily life
- A *clear exploration of the quote*, offering context and meaning

You may notice a number attached to each Pali Canon quote; this corresponds to a *reference list* at the end of the book in the *Bibliography*. I encourage you to seek out the Buddha's words yourself. The original discourses, though ancient, carry a living wisdom that continues to illuminate even now.

What This Book Is (and Is Not)

These are not traditional *Zen koans* [54] that have been passed down from ancient times. You can study such koans from many excellent resources, both online [54] and in print. This book instead offers stories written in the spirit of Zen—clear and subtle. The teachings lie not just between the lines… but within them. Read slowly. Let the story speak to you, even beyond words.

The tone throughout is gentle and unhurried, like a forest walk after rain. You may laugh. You may pause. You may see something you hadn't noticed before.

Each part of the book contains 6 to 7 chapters grouped by theme in 8 parts:

- Calming the Racing Mind
- Letting Go Gracefully
- Managing Emotional Waves
- Building Emotional Resilience
- Listening Beyond Words
- Finding Freedom in Acceptance
- Cultivating Compassion
- Trusting Your Own Way Forward

The stories are designed to take *just 5 minutes to read*, yet they ripple far beyond that.

This book is especially for those who:

- Feel overwhelmed or emotionally stuck
- Want to build mindfulness in everyday moments
- Seek peace, not in grand escapes, but in gentle returns
- Crave stillness, but often get pulled by thought, pressure, or uncertainty

Why the Pali Canon?

The *Pali Canon* [44] is the oldest preserved collection of the Buddha's teachings. It closely mirrors the oral traditions that most authentically reflect the Buddha's own voice—delivered not abstractly, but in response to real people, suffering, and everyday life. While primarily preserved by the Theravāda school, these teachings predate the emergence of sectarian differences and serve as the shared foundation of all Buddhist traditions. They are practical, addressing both monks and laypeople, covering topics such as ethics, meditation, compassion, clarity, the path to liberation, and the daily challenges of life. For this reason, *Whispers of the Zen Forest* continuously revisits these teachings, always approaching them with a beginner's heart.

How to Use This Book

There is no right or wrong way to journey through *Whispers of the Zen Forest*. Let this book meet you wherever you are—over morning tea, beneath the hush of night, or during a moment of pause between your many roles.

- Begin at the start and read one chapter a day
- Flip to any page and let the quote or story call to you
- Keep it by your bedside, your tea table, or your meditation cushion
- Return to a chapter when life feels noisy, and you long to feel still again

Let the rhythm be natural. No pressure. No perfection.

Some days, the reflection will speak louder than the story. Other days, the real-life application will be what you carry into your morning. At times, the story itself will plant a seed that flowers quietly, later.

And when you're ready to go deeper, you'll find a ***short meditation practice*** at the end of every part. These stem from the heart of Zen practice and the Pali Canon and can serve as stepping stones into presence, even amid everyday life.

At first, settling into these *basic* meditations may feel unfamiliar, challenging, or different from your usual practice. That's natural. Like learning to listen in a noisy world, it takes time and effort. But with patience and gentle guidance, the stillness begins to meet you halfway. Over time, you may find yourself interested in exploring more in-depth practices.

The Workbook

To deepen your experience, I've also created a companion:

"Whispers of the Zen Forest Workbook"

This isn't a checklist or academic workbook. It's a space.

This workbook helps you explore the questions posed in the reflection section and record your insights.

Whether you are a beginner on the Zen path, a seasoned student, or simply someone learning to pause, you can use this workbook independently or alongside the book.

Sometimes, writing clarifies what sitting cannot. And sometimes, a question scribbled in a margin becomes the seed of a deeper silence.

And After the Last Page?

You may wonder: *What happens after the last story? Where do I go from here?*

This is where *Yīng Huā Forest* quietly enters, a place where the silence continues.

Born from the same longing that created this book, *Yīng Huā Forest* is a space for those who wish to live with presence. At the end of this book, once you've finished reading, you'll find a gentle guide on how to continue and deepen your own practice.

Why I Wrote This Book

I wrote this as someone who has struggled with noise, both external and internal. Anxiety, burnout, self-doubt… I know their weight. And I also know the relief that came from pausing, listening, and letting the teachings speak.

Writing these stories was not a performance—it was a practice. I did not try to impress the forest. I let it whisper to me.

Now, I extend the same invitation to you.

Why It Matters

In a world that rushes us into proving, posting, chasing, or achieving, *stillness* is a radical act.

To breathe. To notice. To feel what's here without needing to fix it. To come home to yourself without needing to earn it.

These stories are simple, but not shallow. They ask nothing of you except your presence.

May they be your quiet companions in a loud world.

Now, Let's Begin

Find a quiet corner. Open the book wherever you like.

One page. One story. One breath at a time.

Let the forest whisper. And may you remember:

You were never far from peace.

With warmth and gratitude,

Sati

Before You Begin

A Gentle Reminder

In the rush to arrive, we often miss the first step.

In the eagerness to find wisdom, we skip the quiet invitation.

If you've wandered here, ready to read, pause for a breath.

There is an opening before the opening—a soft gate of words that waits not to impress, but to gently welcome you home.

The introduction is that gate.

Simple, steady, and filled with the spirit behind every page that follows.

The introduction is not a formality—it is the first guidance.

A lantern that lights the way before you step forward.

It explains not just *what* this book offers, but *how* it walks hand-in-hand with Zen.

Zen is not a philosophy to be studied with the mind alone.

It is a way of being—simple, direct, unclouded.

And this book, *Whispers of the Zen Forest*, is not merely a book of stories.

It is a practice companion—woven with the essence of Zen.

If you've turned past it—no worries.

Just turn back.

Not as correction, but as care.

Let the journey begin not with haste, but with intention.

Part 1: Calming the Racing Mind

Welcome, Peace Seeker,

Have you ever sat by a river and simply listened—not to the noise, but to the space between sounds? That is where this journey begins.

The mind, left untended, is like a restless wind—whirling with thoughts, memories, regrets, and desires. Like a crowded marketplace at noon, it pulls you in every direction. You may think, *"I must silence this chaos,"* but that is not the Zen way.

We do not battle the wind. We bow to it and sit quietly beneath the tree. We do not chase each thought—we let it pass, like clouds across the moon.

This part of the book is an invitation, not to fix the mind, but to understand it. Not to judge it, but to befriend it. Not to silence it, but to see through it, like sunlight through mist.

Through these stories and reflections, you will meet yourself not as a project to perfect, but as a being learning to return home to your breath, to the earth beneath your feet, and to the moment unfolding now.

Here, you will explore:

- **The Nature of Mental Noise**: How the untrained mind stirs suffering—and how simple awareness can soothe it
- **Teaching Stories of Stillness**: Gentle parables that open the heart and steady the spirit
- **Everyday Mindfulness**: Practical ways to walk with peace, even in a noisy world

So, pause.

Set down your burdens, just for a while. You don't have to make any changes to begin. Just notice what is here. Breathe in. Breathe out. And let's walk gently together into the stillness already waiting within you.

Chapter 1: The Wheel That Waited

Thus, you should train yourselves: 'We will abandon crookedness, faults, & flaws in bodily action. We will abandon crookedness, faults, & flaws in verbal action. We will abandon crookedness, faults, & flaws in mental action.

-The Buddha [2]

In a mountain village, a young craftsman named Riku was eager to prove himself. One day, the old master asked him to carve a wooden wheel.

Riku worked quickly, thinking speed would earn him praise. By sundown, the wheel was finished—shiny, smooth, and ready to roll.

When the master returned, he set Riku's wheel spinning. It clattered and wobbled, then toppled to the ground.

"Tomorrow," the master said gently, "make another."

The next morning, Riku worked slowly. He examined each spoke, listening for the sound of hollowness. He measured the rim again and again, sanding until the wood felt alive beneath his hands.

Days passed. When he finally placed the second wheel before the master, dawn was breaking over the hills.

The old man set it spinning. It rolled straight and true, and then—without falling—stood still, balanced as if on an invisible axle.

Riku felt a quiet joy rise in his chest.

Years later, when younger craftsmen asked how he had learned to make such perfect wheels, he would smile and say:

"A wheel that lasts is the one you don't rush."

Reflection

It's easy to rush through life, chasing quick results and immediate success. We often believe that moving quickly means we are making progress. However, the strength of anything—whether it be work, practice, or character—depends on patience and care. Riku's story reminds us that what we build in haste may spin for a moment, but what we shape with quiet attention can stand steady for a lifetime.

Pause today and ask yourself:

- Where in my life am I rushing to finish instead of taking time to do it well?
- What would it feel like to slow down and give my full presence to each step?
- How might patience transform the quality of what I create?

Even a small task becomes noble when undertaken with a steady and patient heart. When you choose patience over speed, you create something that doesn't just look strong—it endures.

Real-Life Application Example

Scenario: Completing a Report

Imagine you're preparing an important report at work. You feel pressured to finish it quickly so you can move on to the next task.

But you pause and remember the story of the two wheels.

Instead of rushing, you take a little extra time to check your facts, polish your words, and review the details carefully.

When you finally share the report, it's clear, accurate, and well-organized. Your colleagues appreciate the quality, and you feel confident knowing you built it with patience—like the wheel that stands firm.

Exploring the Quote

This quote describes the training of a mind that seeks simplicity and integrity.

It begins with *"Thus, you should train yourselves."* This is an invitation to practice, not to accept ideas passively. True change is cultivated through steady effort.

"We will abandon crookedness, faults, and flaws in bodily action." This points to making the body an instrument of kindness and honesty. No harmful deeds, no hidden agendas.

"We will abandon crookedness, faults, and flaws in verbal action." Words can heal or wound. Here is the resolve to speak clearly, truthfully, and without malice.

"We will abandon crookedness, faults, and flaws in mental action." This is the root. A mind free from greed, ill will, and delusion becomes spacious and unburdened.

In simple terms, training the body, speech, and mind to be straight and clear is the ground where peace can grow.

Chapter 2: The Softest Bed

Always, always, he sleeps in ease:

The Brahman totally unbound, who doesn't adhere to sensual pleasures, who's without acquisitions & cooled.

Having cut all ties & subdued fear in the heart, calmed,

He sleeps in ease, having reached peace of awareness.

-The Buddha [3]

In a little mountain temple, a young monk named Haru spent the winter grumbling about the cold.

Every night, he layered on extra blankets, piled straw around his mat, and huddled close to the brazier. Still, he felt restless, unable to sleep.

One morning, he confessed to the old abbot, "Master, no matter what I do, I can't find comfort. The wind seems to find me anyway."

The abbot nodded, his eyes bright with kindness. "Tonight, Haru, do one thing differently. Before you lie down, sweep your mind as carefully as you sweep your floor."

That evening, Haru did as he was told. He sat in stillness, watching each thought drift by—regret, longing, irritation—and gently let them go. When he lay down, the wind still howled outside, and the floor was still cold beneath him. Yet for the first time all winter, his heart felt light. He slept peacefully until dawn.

In the morning, he bowed to the abbot. "Last night," he said softly, "I discovered the softest bed is the one made of a quiet mind."

Reflection

We often believe comfort comes from having everything just right—warmth, safety, and pleasant conditions. But even in the coldest, harshest place, a calm mind brings real ease.

When the fires of craving, anger, and confusion are gone, peace arises naturally. Proper rest doesn't depend on the softness of the bed but on the softness of the heart.

Pause today and ask yourself:

- When have I looked for comfort in external things instead of tending to my own mind?
- What "fires" of craving, anger, or confusion could I begin to let go of?
- How might I create a sense of calm no matter what is happening around me?

Even though saving ourselves from the cold is wise and physical safety is necessary, the same care should be given to our minds. Just as we shelter the body, we must also protect the mind—clearing it of restlessness and tending it with patience and understanding.

Real-Life Application Example

Scenario: Struggling to Relax After a Stressful Day

Imagine you've had a long, difficult day. You return home exhausted, but when you lie down, your mind keeps replaying old frustrations.

You remember Haru in the temple.

Instead of adding more distractions—scrolling on your phone, reaching for another snack—you sit quietly, noticing each thought as it arises. You don't judge it or follow it. You simply watch and release. After a few minutes, your breath feels deeper. Your shoulders soften. You lie down again, and though nothing around you has changed, you find that sleep comes easily—because inside, everything is finally at rest.

Exploring the Quote

This quote describes the profound ease of one who has fully let go.

It begins with *"Always, always, he sleeps in ease."* A mind free of clinging rests in peace at all times, undisturbed by regrets or cravings.

"The Brahman totally unbound, who doesn't adhere to sensual pleasures, who's without acquisitions and cooled." This is a person who no longer chases pleasures or collects possessions. The fires of wanting have gone out, leaving the heart calm and cool.

"Having cut all ties and subdued fear in the heart, calmed." All attachments have been released. Fear no longer has a place to take root. The heart is steady and fearless.

"He sleeps in ease, having reached peace of awareness." Even in sleep, there is no disturbance. Awareness is settled, tranquil, and free.

In simple terms, when nothing is grasped, life becomes light. Rest is natural, like a quiet pond undisturbed by any wind.

Chapter 3: The Cup and the River

Suppose you say: 'No matter how this person performs a deed, they experience it the same way.' This being so, the spiritual life could not be lived, and there'd be no chance of making a complete end of suffering.

Suppose you say: 'No matter how this person performs a deed, they experience the result as it should be experienced.' This being so, the spiritual life can be lived, and there is a chance of making a complete end of suffering.

-The Buddha [7]

A young student named Yuki once came to the old Zen teacher, eyes full of worry.

"Master," she said, "I made a mistake. I spoke harshly to my friend, and now I can't stop feeling terrible. My heart is heavy like a stone."

The teacher filled a small cup with water. Into it, he dropped a handful of salt. "Taste this," he said.

Yuki sipped and made a face. "It's so bitter!"

Then he led her to the river flowing past the temple. He scattered the same salt into the water and cupped some in his hands.

"Now taste."

She drank and smiled in surprise. "It's fresh!"

The teacher looked at her kindly.

"Your mistake is like the salt," he said. "If you hold it in a small mind, it will always taste bitter. But if you hold it in a vast heart, it dissolves into something much larger."

From that day on, whenever Yuki felt regret rise, she would walk to the river, watch it flow, and remember:

I can make my heart as wide as this.

Reflection

When we do something unskillful, our first instinct is often to shrink into shame. We replay the mistake again and again, believing we must be as small and unworthy as our worst moment.

However, it isn't the salt that poisons the cup—it's the cup's size. A heart trained in compassion and wisdom becomes like a river. It can hold sorrow without becoming bitter.

Pause today and ask yourself:

- Where am I holding a mistake in a small, tight mind?
- What would it feel like to let my heart grow wider?
- How can I cultivate kindness towards myself so that this regret can dissolve?

When the heart is vast, no single fault can define you.

Real-Life Application Example

Scenario: Feeling Overwhelmed by a Small Mistake at Work

Imagine you sent an email with an error that embarrassed you. All day, you replay it in your mind, feeling smaller and smaller.

You remember Yuki and the river.

Instead of tightening around your guilt, you take a walk, breathing deeply. You remind yourself: *I am more than this one moment.*

Back at your desk, you send a simple apology and correction. As you do, you feel the bitterness begin to fade—like salt dissolving into a river that keeps on flowing.

Exploring the Quote

This quote describes the living truth of how actions bear their consequences.

It begins with *"No matter how this person performs a deed, they experience it the same way."* This is the view that karma unfolds in a rigid, mechanical way. It does not matter what you intended or how you held your heart—everything is predetermined, unchanging.

"The spiritual life could not be lived, and there'd be no chance of making a complete end of suffering." If things were this fixed, practice would be in vain. No reflection, no mindfulness, no effort could touch the result.

Then comes a deeper understanding: *"No matter how this person performs a deed, they experience the result as it should be experienced."* Here, karma ripens according to many conditions—intention, awareness, circumstances, and the presence of understanding.

"The spiritual life can be lived, and there is a chance of making a complete end of suffering." Because results are shaped by how we meet them, the path is open. We can change, soften, and free the heart.

In simple terms, when you see that karma is not a prison but a field of conditions, you discover the quiet possibility of freedom.

Chapter 4: The Gift That Was Never Taken

One should not consider the faults of others, nor their doing or not doing good or bad deeds. One should consider only whether one has done or not done good or bad deeds.

-The Buddha [21]

In a small Zen temple by the sea, a young monk named Kento was sweeping the courtyard when an angry villager stormed in.

"You lazy fool!" the man shouted. "You eat rice from our fields and do nothing of worth!" His voice thundered. His insults were sharp as nettles.

Kento paused. He bowed his head respectfully but said nothing.

After a while, the villager, exhausted by his own rage, demanded, "Well? Have you nothing to say for yourself?"

The old abbot, who had been watching quietly from the doorway, stepped forward. He smiled gently. "If someone offers you a gift," he said, "and you do not take it—who does it belong to?"

The villager frowned. "To the one who brought it."

"Just so," the abbot replied.

The courtyard grew still. Kento bowed again.

Reflection

When someone's anger erupts, our first instinct is to defend, explain, or retaliate. But another's fury does not have to become our burden.

Kento's story reminds us that insults are like gifts. If we refuse to pick them up, they never enter our hands.

Pause today and ask yourself:

- When have I accepted someone's anger as my own?
- What would happen if I simply let their words pass by, like leaves on a stream?
- How might my mind feel if I stopped carrying what was never mine?

A heart that stays open, but does not cling, is unshakable.

Real-Life Application Example

Scenario: Facing Criticism Without Reacting

Imagine a coworker criticizes you sharply in front of others. You feel the heat rise in your chest, your mind scrambling for a defense.

You remember Kento standing quietly in the courtyard.

You take a slow breath. Instead of arguing, you let the words pass without picking them up.

Later, you reflect calmly on whether there is any truth in them. The rest, you leave behind.

And as you walk away, you feel light, knowing you don't have to carry every burden that is offered to you.

Exploring the Quote

This quote describes the practice of turning one's attention inward rather than outward. It begins with *"One should not consider the faults of others."* This is a gentle reminder to stop measuring and judging others for their mistakes.

"Nor their doing or not doing good or bad deeds." It is easy to become preoccupied with other people's choices, praising or blaming. This habit only distracts and stirs the mind.

"One should consider only whether one has done or not done good or bad deeds." The real work is to look honestly at your own heart. Reflection becomes clear when you see your actions as they are, without excuses or comparisons.

In simple terms, peace grows when you stop looking outward for faults and start tending to your own garden within.

Chapter 5: The Farmer and the Snake of Greed

That deed is not well done, if one has to repent for having done it, and if, with a tearful face, one has to weep as a result of that deed.

-The Buddha [22]

In a quiet village, a young man named Jiro spent his days gathering firewood.

One morning, as he walked the forest path, he noticed the old Zen teacher standing near a pile of fallen branches.

The teacher looked down calmly and said, “Ah, do you see that snake?”

Jiro peered closer but saw only tangled leaves. “Master, I don’t see any snake.”

“Be watchful,” the teacher replied, and continued on his way.

Curious, Jiro began to move the branches aside. Beneath them, he discovered a leather pouch, heavy with gold coins.

His heart thumped in his chest. *If I take this, no one will know,* he thought. But then he remembered the teacher’s voice: *Do you see that snake?*

He felt his desire cool. Instead of taking the pouch, he left it where it was and returned to his work with an easy heart.

Years later, when asked why he never regretted anything he did, Jiro would smile and say: “Because I learned to look twice before I reached out my hand.”

Reflection

Sometimes temptation comes disguised as opportunity. It can look harmless—even lucky. But unexamined desire is like a snake beneath the leaves.

Jiro’s story reminds us that when we pause to look twice, we protect ourselves from regret. True wisdom isn’t about never feeling desire—it’s about seeing clearly before we act.

Pause today and ask yourself:

- Where in my life am I tempted to act without reflection?
- What would it feel like to pause and look more closely?

- How might my mind feel if I chose only what I could carry with a clear heart?

A moment of awareness can save years of sorrow.

Real-Life Application Example

Scenario: Feeling Tempted to Bend the Rules at Work

Imagine you discover a way to claim extra expenses no one would likely notice. Your heart races with the thought of easy gain.

You remember Jiro and the hidden snake.

Before you act, you take a slow breath and ask yourself: *Will this leave me proud or ashamed tomorrow?*

You decide to leave the temptation untouched.

As you walk away, you feel lightness in your chest—a quiet relief that comes from choosing what you won't have to regret later.

Exploring the Quote

This quote describes how to discern whether an action is truly wholesome.

It begins with *"That deed is not well done, if one has to repent for having done it."* When an action leaves a feeling of regret in the heart, it is a sign that it was rooted in confusion or harm.

"And if, with a tearful face, one has to weep as a result of that deed." Actions that bring sorrow and remorse reveal themselves as unskillful by the suffering they leave behind.

This teaching offers a simple measure: observe how you feel afterward. Peace is the mark of what is wise.

In simple terms, a good deed is one you can remember without regret, like a clear sky that needs no covering.

Chapter 6: The Treasure Beneath the Dust

If a person is energetic, mindful, pure in his thought, word and deed, and if he does everything with care and consideration, restrains his senses, earns his living according to the Law (Dhamma) and is not unheedful, then, the fame and fortune of that mindful person steadily increase.

-The Buddha [20]

In a quiet town, a young man named Hiro returned after a long absence. When he was a boy, his family had hidden their wealth beneath a stone in the courtyard, telling him: "Leave it there until your heart is ready."

Now grown and alone, Hiro knelt by the old stone. When he lifted it, the gold gleamed in the morning sun.

But as he reached for it, a question rose in his mind:

What good is treasure if it costs me my peace?

He lowered the stone again.

For many months, he lived simply—mending baskets, sweeping courtyards, and greeting each dawn with gratitude.

One morning, the village elder passed by Hiro's doorway and heard his calm, steady voice greeting the dawn. He paused, listening with quiet curiosity.

"That is no ordinary voice," he thought.

Later, when the elder learned the truth about Hiro's past and the hidden gold, he nodded with respect.

"You waited without greed," he said gently. "That is why your treasure is yours without shame."

Hiro bowed low, feeling a warmth in his chest.

In that moment, he understood: the years of patience and simple living had made him richer than any fortune ever could.

Reflection

When life offers us something valuable, our first impulse is often to grasp it quickly, afraid it will slip away. But the true wealth is not in having—it is in knowing when to wait and when to act with a clear mind.

Hiro's story reminds us that patience and honesty create a foundation no fear can shake. What we claim with integrity will never turn into a burden.

Pause today and ask yourself:

- Where am I tempted to take something before the right time?
- What would happen if I trusted that what is meant for me will return in its own season?
- How might my heart feel if I chose patience over haste?

A quiet mind is the greatest treasure of all.

Real-Life Application Example

Scenario: Waiting for Recognition in Your Career

Imagine you've been working hard, unnoticed, while others are promoted ahead of you. You feel the urge to push, to prove yourself, to demand acknowledgment.

You remember Hiro lifting the stone but choosing to wait.

Instead of acting out of fear, you continue to do your work with care and steadiness. You trust that your effort will find its place when the time is right.

Perhaps recognition comes. Perhaps it doesn't.

Then, months later, a round of layoffs occurs. To your quiet relief, your position is safe. You realize that even if you weren't the loudest voice in the room, your steady presence and respectful relationships mattered.

Maybe it wasn't about being the most visible. Perhaps it was about being trusted, being reliable, and being someone others were glad to have around.

And as you sit with this, you feel a quiet assurance that something good has already come from your patience—something more profound than any title or applause.

Exploring the Quote

This quote describes the qualities that enable a life to flourish naturally.

It begins with *"If a person is energetic, mindful, pure in his thought, word, and deed."* Energy means steady effort. Mindfulness keeps the heart present. Purity brings honesty and harmlessness into every part of life.

"And if he does everything with care and consideration." This is the art of not rushing. Each action is done with attention and respect.

"Restrains his senses." The mind is not pulled away by craving for sights, sounds, and pleasures. It remains steady and clear.

"Earns his living according to the Law (Dhamma) and is not unheedful." Livelihood is honest. Awareness does not drift into forgetfulness.

In simple terms, when you live with energy, care, and integrity, respect and good fortune grow quietly, like a tree nourished by good roots.

Practice Meditation: The Wheel of Stillness

1. **Settle.**

Sit upright—grounded, relaxed, alert. Let your hands rest gently. Allow the body to be still like a quiet wheel, unmoving yet alive.

2. **Breathe**

Breathe through your nose. Inhale. Exhale. Continue inhaling and exhaling normally. Let the breath be your anchor.

3. **Notice the Mind.**

If thoughts arise and carry you away, notice them—like clouds drifting across the sky. Gently return to the breath and begin again. No judgment. Just return.

4. **Let It Be.**

If a persistent thought or feeling arises, pause and acknowledge it. Let it be seen, but do not chase it. Rest with it, without clinging. When it softens, return to the breath.

5. **Just This.**

Be still. Be present. Nothing to fix. Nowhere to go. Just this breath. Just this moment. The wheel waits not to rush, but to remain.

6. **End Gently.**

After a few minutes (or as long as you like), slowly bring awareness back to your body. Bow softly to the stillness you met within.

Part 2: Letting Go Gracefully

Hello again, Quiet Friend,

The leaf does not resist the wind. It does not ask why it must fall, nor does it cling to the branch. It simply lets go, trusting that the earth will receive it. We are also encouraged to live in this way.

Yet the human heart often clings—not out of ignorance, but out of love, memory, fear, or habit. We hold tight to what once gave us meaning: roles we've outgrown, relationships that have shifted, dreams that no longer fit the person we are becoming. But here is the gentle truth the Dharma teaches: *Letting go is not rejection. It is a return.* Return to simplicity. Return to trust. Return to the spaciousness of what is here now.

This part of the journey invites you into that sacred pause—the breath before holding on, the breath before releasing. You'll meet stories where sorrow softens, where burdens are seen for what they are, and where peace comes not from grasping, but from allowing.

You are not asked to let go all at once. Only to loosen your grip. Only to see clearly. Only to ask: *"Do I still need to carry this?"*

Here's what you'll explore:

- **The Nature of Release**: Why clinging brings suffering and how wise surrender leads to inner freedom
- **Stories of Unburdening**: Real and reflective tales that shine a light on the path of release
- **Practices to Soften and Trust**: Gentle invitations to meet your own letting go with patience, not pressure

So now, sit quietly. Feel the weight you've carried—lovingly, bravely, long enough.

Let the next page be like the open sky. Let's walk gently onward.

Chapter 7: The Empty Cup

Death comes to all beings; before their desires are satiated,

death takes them away.

-The Buddha [24]

In a quiet temple on the city's outskirts, a woman named Mei arrived one morning, carrying an urn pressed to her chest. Her face was hollow with sorrow.

"Master," she whispered to the old monk sweeping the courtyard, "my husband has died. I beg you—tell me how to end this pain."

The monk set down his broom and poured her a cup of tea. "Drink," he said softly.

She took a sip and wept. "Even the taste of tea feels bitter."

"Then go," he told her, "and bring me a cup of clear water for the tea from a well that has never reflected the face of grief."

Mei bowed and walked from the temple. She visited every well in the town, asking the same question: "Have you drawn water here without sorrow ever falling across it?"

The old potter shook his head. "I cried into this well when my wife died."

The young mother looked away. "I came here when my baby was ill."

By sunset, Mei's feet were dusty, and her heart was heavy, but her mind had grown still. She saw that her grief was no different from theirs. She was not alone.

When she returned to the temple, the monk asked, "Did you find the water?"

"No," she said quietly. "But I found the truth."

The monk nodded and poured her another cup of tea. "Drink again," he said.

Mei lifted the cup to her lips. This time, the tea tasted warm and clear.

The monk looked into her eyes. "When you let go of believing your pain is yours alone," he said gently, "the bitterness leaves the cup."

Mei held the cup close, feeling—for the first time—a small, steady peace rising in her chest.

Reflection

When grief comes, it feels like no one has ever suffered as you do. The world becomes small, your heart sealed tight around sorrow.

But Mei's story reminds us that grief is part of the great river that connects every living being. When you see that your pain is not separate, something softens inside.

The tea is the same. Only your heart has changed.

Pause today and ask yourself:

- Where am I clinging to the idea that my suffering is unique?
- What happens if I let my heart open to the truth that everyone carries some form of loss?
- How might my pain feel different if I stopped resisting it?

When you let go of isolation, you make space for compassion—for yourself and for all beings.

Real-Life Application Example

Scenario: Feeling Isolated After a Major Disappointment

Imagine you've poured your heart into a project, a dream, or a relationship, and it falls apart. You wake each morning with a heavy ache, believing no one could possibly understand how much it hurts.

One evening, you decide to attend a local support group at the community center—just to sit quietly among others who are also facing life's upheavals.

As people begin to share, you hear stories of heartbreak, of losing loved ones, of starting over after everything seemed lost.

Little by little, something shifts. You feel your sadness soften. You see it not as a private curse, but as a bond that connects you to every person in the circle.

Later that night, you walk home under the quiet sky. You still feel the ache, but it is no longer so sharp.

And as you breathe in the cool air, you realize you are not alone, and in that simple truth, something tender and steady begins to grow.

Exploring the Quote

This quote describes the simple, unchanging truth of impermanence.
It begins with *"Death comes to all beings."* No creature, no person, escapes the ending of the body. This is part of the natural order.
"Before their desires are satiated." Even as people chase pleasures, achievements, and dreams, craving is never truly satisfied.
"Death takes them away." Life ends often before longing is fulfilled. Nothing can be clung to forever.
In simple terms, remembering that death comes while desires remain unfinished invites us to live wisely now, appreciating what is here without grasping.

Chapter 8: The Arrow That Never Flew

If there is no wound on the hand, one may handle poison; poison does not affect one who has no wound; there can be no evil for one who has no evil intention.

-The Buddha [25]

In a quiet village near the edge of a great forest, there lived a hunter named Tama. Every dawn, he set out with his bow, determined to fill his basket.

One morning, he spotted a small deer grazing by a banyan tree. He drew his bow, steady and sure. But as he took aim, a soft voice within him whispered:

Is this all you were made for?

Startled, he hesitated.

He felt the stillness of the trees around him. In that silence, he sensed that life was not something to be claimed or defended—it was something shared.

He lowered the bow.

For the first time, he noticed how the morning light caught in the deer's eyes, how the breath of the forest moved through him too.

He set the arrow gently on the ground.

Years later, when villagers asked why he had abandoned the hunt, he would smile and say:

"The greatest catch of my life was the moment I stopped aiming."

Reflection

We often think strength means never hesitating, never questioning. But the quietest moment of pause can reveal a deeper wisdom.

The hunter's story shows us that a single breath of awareness can change the entire course of a life. The urge to harm, the need to prove, the habit to possess—all of it can soften when we simply look and see.

Pause today and ask yourself:

- Where am I aiming without thinking?

- What would happen if I lowered my "arrow" and looked more closely?
- How might my life open if I stopped fighting and started listening?

Sometimes the most powerful choice is the one that leaves no wound behind.

Real-Life Application Example

Scenario: Responding to Conflict Without Striking Back

Imagine a colleague criticizes you sharply in a meeting. You feel your body tense. Words rise like arrows on the string—ready to defend, ready to wound.

Then you remember Tama in the forest.

You take a breath. Instead of firing back, you pause. You feel the space around your reaction.

In that space, you choose a calmer response. You ask, "Can you help me understand what's bothering you?"

The tension in the room softens. The conversation shifts.

And you leave the meeting with no regrets—only the quiet strength of the arrow that never flew.

Exploring the Quote

This quote describes the protective power of a pure heart.

It begins with *"If there is no wound on the hand, one may handle poison."* When there is no cut, poison cannot enter. The hand remains unharmed.

"Poison does not affect one who has no wound." Similarly, harmful things cannot penetrate where there is no opening.

"There can be no evil for one who has no evil intention." When the mind is free of ill will, greed, and deceit, unwholesome influences cannot take root.

In simple terms, a mind without malice is like unbroken skin—nothing harmful can truly touch it.

Chapter 9: The Bundle at the Gate

Your letting go of it will be for your long-term happiness & benefit... Whatever arises in dependence on intellect-contact, experienced either as pleasure, as pain, or as neither-pleasure-nor-pain, that too is not yours: let go of it.

-The Buddha [47]

In a quiet mountain village, a young monk named Taro came to the old Zen teacher with a troubled heart.

"Master," he said, bowing low, "I feel burdened by every thought, every feeling, every wish. My mind is full, and none of it brings peace."

The teacher led Taro to the temple gate, where a large bundle of straw lay tied with twine.

"Lift it," the teacher instructed.

Taro picked up the bundle. It was heavy, awkward against his chest.

"Now carry it to the far wall."

Step by step, Taro struggled across the courtyard, sweat gathering on his brow.

At last, he set it down. He looked to the teacher, expecting praise.

But the old man simply asked, "Whose bundle is that?"

Taro blinked. "I don't know. It isn't mine."

"Then why," the teacher said gently, "are you carrying it?"

Taro stood in silence.

The teacher smiled and placed a hand on his shoulder.

"Thoughts, feelings, even this body—they arise and pass. None of them belongs to you. You can notice them. You can set them down."

Taro felt the strain in his arms ease. And in that moment, he understood: all the heaviness he carried was no more his than a bundle of straw left at the gate.

Reflection

How much of what you carry—worries, regrets, ideas about who you are—was never truly yours?

Even the body and the mind are like grass and twigs in a grove: they arise, change, and pass away. When you cling to them as "mine," suffering grows heavy. When you see them as passing bundles, you are free to set them down.

Taro's story reminds us that peace begins the moment you stop holding onto what was never yours to begin with. Every moment offers you the chance to put the bundle down.

Pause today and ask yourself:

- What thoughts or feelings am I clinging to as "mine"?
- How would it feel to simply observe them without ownership?
- What might lighten if I let them go, even for a breath?

Real-Life Application Example

Scenario: Carrying Criticism from Work

Imagine your boss criticizes your work in a meeting. All day, the words replay in your mind: *I'm not good enough. I've failed. Everyone thinks poorly of me.*

You feel tightness in your chest, as if you are carrying a heavy load, and you can't put it down.

That evening, you sit quietly and remember Taro and the bundle.

You ask yourself, *Are these words truly mine? Or are they just sounds and thoughts passing through awareness?*

You take a slow breath. You notice how the criticism came, stayed a while, and now begins to fade.

With each exhale, the bundle feels a little lighter.

And as you open your eyes, you sense freedom and lightness.

Exploring the Quote

This quote describes the freedom that comes from not clinging to fleeting experiences.

It begins with *"Your letting go of it will be for your long-term happiness and benefit."* Release is not loss. Letting go brings peace that endures.

"Whatever arises in dependence on intellect-contact." Thoughts, feelings, and perceptions appear when the mind meets its objects.

"Experienced either as pleasure, as pain, or as neither-pleasure-nor-pain." All experiences can be categorized into three simple tones: pleasant, unpleasant, and neutral.

"That too is not yours: let go of it." None of it is truly who you are. Clinging only creates struggle.

In simple terms, when you stop claiming every thought and feeling as "mine," you find a spacious ease that cannot be disturbed.

Chapter 10: The Lantern That Would Not Stay Lit

Nothing is worth insisting on.

-The Buddha [16]

One evening, the young monk Ryo sat in meditation beneath the old plum tree. He had promised himself he would stay awake until dawn, determined to meet his restless mind with unwavering stillness.

But as the night deepened, his eyelids grew heavy. His head drooped. He jerked awake, only to sink again into drowsy darkness.

At last, Master Shun appeared, lantern in hand. He set the lantern on the ground beside Ryo and said, "Ah, I see your flame is flickering."

Ryo lowered his eyes. "Master, no matter how hard I try, I keep falling asleep."

The old man smiled. "Then try something different."

He sat down beside him and spoke softly:

"When the mind grows dull, do not fight it with more force. Instead, bring gentle curiosity."

He gestured to the lantern. "When the flame weakens, do you scold it? No. You trim the wick, clear the glass, feed it air."

Ryo looked up. "But how do I trim the wick of the mind?"

Master Shun counted on his fingers:

"Change the focus of your attention. Reflect on the teachings. Speak them aloud. Stand and walk slowly. Wash your face in cold water. Look up at the night sky. Fill your thoughts with brightness. And if the flame still fades, lie down mindfully and promise yourself you will rise again."

Ryo felt his weariness ease. He bowed low.

"And remember," Master Shun added, "when you see that nothing is worth clinging to—not even this fatigue—your mind becomes like a lantern that never goes out."

That night, Ryo practiced each method with patience.

By dawn, his heart was clear and bright, as if the sky itself had taken root inside him.

Reflection

When your energy falters, it is easy to scold yourself or give up in frustration. But just as a lantern's flame needs tending, the mind needs gentle care when it grows dull. Fatigue is not a failure. It is a signal. When you meet it with curiosity rather than judgment, you discover that wakefulness can be rekindled again and again.

This is how letting go begins: not by forcing yourself to be different, but by allowing what is here and responding wisely. Each time you soften your grip on blame or resistance, you create space for clarity to return on its own.

Ryo's story reminds us that no effort is wasted. Each time you adjust your posture, shift your focus, or simply breathe with awareness, you are feeding the flame of presence—and releasing the heaviness that comes from clinging to struggle.

Pause today and ask yourself:

- When I feel tired or discouraged, how do I usually respond?
- What would it feel like to meet my weariness with patience instead of blame?
- Which simple action—standing, washing my face, lifting my gaze—could help me let go of frustration and rediscover calm?

Real-Life Application Example

Scenario: Losing Focus While Working or Studying

Imagine you've been working at your desk for hours. Your eyelids grow heavy. Words blur on the screen. A dull fog settles over your thoughts.

Instead of pushing yourself harder or sinking into frustration, you pause.

You stand, stretch your body slowly, and take three steady breaths. You walk to the window and look up at the sky, letting your eyes rest in the vastness.

You splash cool water on your face, return to your chair, and feel the shift—subtle but unmistakable. Your mind is clearer. The heaviness has softened.

In that moment, you realize why this works: by stepping away, you stopped clinging to the demand to be endlessly productive. You let go of the judgment that you were failing. And in releasing that grip, you made room for presence and calm to naturally return.

It isn't just about waking up. It's about remembering you don't have to force yourself to keep carrying what makes you weary.

Exploring the Quote

This quote originates describes the heart of letting go.

It begins simply with *"Nothing is worth insisting on."* No idea, feeling, or possession truly lasts. Clinging only creates tension and sorrow. The mind opens when it sees that clinging to anything—ideas, feelings, possessions—brings suffering.

When you stop insisting on being right, on having more, on holding what must change, the mind becomes light.

This teaching invites a soft, spacious way of being. Nothing needs to be grasped so tightly.

In simple terms, peace comes when you let life flow without demanding it be any particular way.

Chapter 11: The Bowl on the River

One indeed is one's own refuge; how can others be a refuge to one? With oneself thoroughly tamed, one can attain a refuge, which is so difficult to attain.

-The Buddha [29]

In a small mountain temple, a nun named Hana lived. Before she shaved her head and donned her gray robes, she had been a potter. Her hands had shaped hundreds of bowls—some plain, some painted, all made with care.

But among them, there was one bowl she loved above all. It was the very first she had crafted as a girl: simple clay, fired unevenly, but precious to her heart.

When Hana joined the temple, she brought that old bowl with her. Every morning, she filled it with water and placed it in front of the Buddha's image.

Years passed, and Hana's devotion deepened. Yet whenever she looked at the bowl, she felt a quiet pull in her chest—an ache she couldn't name.

One summer morning, the Zen master visited her cell. He noticed the bowl and lifted it gently.

"This bowl," he asked, "who does it belong to?"

"It is mine," Hana whispered. "I made it."

The Zen master nodded. "And who are you?"

Hana looked down, her heart beating fast.

After a long silence, she said, "No one."

"Then why does no one still carry such a burden?" he asked softly.

That evening, Hana walked alone to the river. The sky was violet with dusk. She set the bowl on the water. For a moment, it floated, catching the last light—then slowly, it filled and sank. Tears blurred her eyes, but she did not look away.

When she returned to the temple, her hands felt strangely light. For the first time, she understood that letting go was not losing—it was returning to the freedom she had carried all along.

Reflection

Sometimes, we cling to what we love most without realizing how much it weighs on us. Even something beautiful—a treasured memory, a success, a role, an identity—can become a hidden burden.

Hana's story reminds us that letting go is not about rejecting what we have valued; it's about embracing what we have learned. It is about loosening our grip so our hearts can breathe again.

Letting go doesn't mean you no longer care. It means you no longer cling. And in that softening, you find a freedom that cannot be broken.

Pause today and ask yourself:

- What am I still carrying that I no longer need to hold so tightly?
- Who would I be if I placed this burden gently down?
- What small step could I take to release one old attachment and trust what remains?

Real-Life Application Example

Scenario: Moving On from an Old Role or Identity

Imagine you have worked for years in a role that defined you, perhaps as a manager, a founder, or a parent whose children are now grown. You take pride in it. You feel safe inside it.

Then the time comes to step away.

At first, you might feel lost, like Hana standing alone by the river, unsure of who you are without the old title or story.

But when you give yourself permission to let go—gently, without self-judgment—you discover that what you loved is not truly gone. The skills, the care, the lessons remain, but the weight of clinging does not.

And in that moment, your heart feels light again, ready to meet the next chapter with fresh curiosity, unburdened by what used to be.

Exploring the Quote

This quote describes the strength that comes from inner self-reliance.
It begins with *"One indeed is one's own refuge; how can others be a refuge to one?"* No one else can do your inner work. Relying only on others for peace or freedom leads to disappointment.
"With oneself thoroughly tamed." When the mind is trained to be calm, clear, and steady, it becomes a safe place.
"One can attain a refuge, which is so difficult to attain." This unshakable refuge is a quiet heart, free from confusion and fear.
In simple terms, lasting security is not found outside of oneself. It grows within when you patiently train and care for your own mind.

Chapter 12: The Cup with No Handle

People follow & associate for a motive.
Friends without a motive these days are rare.
They're shrewd for their own ends, & impure.
Wander alone like a rhinoceros.
-The Buddha [46]

A wandering man named Kazuo stopped by a potter's hut to rest. The potter, a man named Soma, greeted him warmly.

"Will you stay for tea?" Soma asked, already pouring hot water over leaves.

Kazuo bowed. "Only a moment."

As the tea steamed, Soma brought out a fine clay cup—but with no handle.

"Strange cup," Kazuo noted gently.

Soma grinned. "It teaches me. A cup with a handle invites grasping. One without reminds me to hold carefully, with full attention—and to let go without clinging."

Kazuo nodded, eyes glinting. "People, too, are often grasped like handled cups—expected to offer comfort, reward, or usefulness."

Soma sighed. "It's hard these days. Everyone seems to want something."

Kazuo looked out toward the misty woods.

"When one walks alone," he said, "it's not out of bitterness, but clarity. Better to walk alone than carry the weight of half-held friendships and transactional smiles."

Soma placed the cup in Kazuo's hands. "Still, it feels good to share tea with someone who isn't reaching for anything."

Kazuo smiled. "Then for this moment, we're not alone."

They drank in silence.

Reflection

Sometimes, what we long for most is companionship free of conditions—where we are not expected to perform, produce, or please. But in a world woven with transactions and unspoken expectations, such friendship can feel rare, like the cup without a handle.

Kazuo's story reminds us that solitude is not always loneliness. It can be a path of integrity—a gentle refusal to be pulled by hidden motives or tangled obligations. When we no longer reach to grasp or be grasped, we discover a quiet strength in simply *being*.

Letting go of clinging to roles and relationships doesn't mean closing the heart. It means walking without neediness. It means offering presence like tea—warm, unforced, and easy to set down. And when someone meets us there, not to take or demand, but simply to be… Then, we are no longer alone.

Pause and ask yourself:

- Are my connections rooted in shared presence or silent expectation?
- Can I sit with someone without needing to impress, fix, or be understood?
- Where might I walk more freely if I stopped grasping?

Real-Life Application Example

Scenario: Feeling Used in a Friendship

Imagine you have a friend who only calls when they need something—help moving, advice, a listening ear. You offer, again and again. But afterward, silence. No check-in. No warmth unless there's a request.

At first, you feel hurt. Maybe even resentful. But instead of reacting with anger or cutting them off abruptly, you pause.

You remember Kazuo's words: *"It's not out of bitterness, but clarity."*

So, you begin to shift. You stop reaching. You stop over-giving. You let the silence arrive without rushing to fill it.

If the friend reaches out again, you greet them kindly, but without attachment. You no longer expect their calls to be different. You've released the handle.

And in that release, you free yourself—not from people, but from the ache of needing something they cannot offer.

Your solitude becomes a sanctuary, not a punishment.

And when someone does show up, just to sit beside you without reaching for anything? You will know what it's worth. And you will hold it gently.

Exploring the Quote

This teaching comes from a series of verses that celebrate the beauty of solitude and self-reliance on the path.

It begins with *"People follow and associate for a motive."* Often, relationships are formed based on gain, advantage, or hidden desires—not always from a genuine place.

"Friends without a motive these days are rare." It's uncommon to find those who connect with no expectation, no agenda—just simple presence and goodwill.

"They're shrewd for their own ends, and impure." Many are clever with words and smiles, yet their intentions are self-serving or clouded by attachment and ego.

"Wander alone like a rhinoceros." Not as a rejection of the world, but as a reminder: better to walk alone in truth than be entangled in hollow company.

In simple terms, walk your path with clarity. Let solitude be your companion when company pulls you away from peace. When you are rooted within, even alone, you are never lost.

Practice Meditation: The Practice of Letting Go

1. **Sit with Softness.**

Take your seat—stable, relaxed, upright. Let the hands rest. Gently soften your gaze or close your eyes. Let the body be still, like a cup placed gently on the earth.

2. **Breathe & Feel.**

Breathe in through the nose. Feel the breath arrive at the nostrils, then leave. There is nothing to change—only to notice.

With each exhale, let go of fixing. Let go of holding. Let go of the need to be whole.

3. **Watch the Mind.**

Thoughts may rise—memories, plans, worries. You do not need to chase or judge them. Gently return to the breath and feel its presence around the nostrils.

4. **Sit with the Crack.**

If an emotion arises—such as grief, anger, or fear—do not push it away. Allow it to sit beside you, like a cracked cup still capable of holding space. You don't need to repair it. You only need to be present. Observe it as you observe your breath.

5. **Rest in Openness.**

Let this moment be as it is—imperfect, quiet, complete in its incompleteness. There is nothing missing. There is only now. Remain aware of the breath around the nostrils.

6. **Close Softly.**

When you're ready, breathe in deeply once more. Bow to the crack, the stillness, the breath.

You are not broken. You are becoming.

Part 3: Managing Emotional Waves

Hello, Inner Wanderer,

Emotions rise like tides—sometimes a soft ripple, sometimes a crashing wave. And in their swell, we often forget that the ocean has a stillness beneath it.

Anger, grief, shame, restlessness—these are not flaws in the human design. They are part of the weather of the heart. But we were never meant to be swept away by them. We were meant to learn how to float.

This part of the path is not about controlling or avoiding what you feel. It is about learning to sit with it, breathe through it, and listen without being undone. When you slow down and meet what stirs within you with curiosity—not judgment—you open a gate to deep wisdom.

These stories and reflections will not ask you to deny your rage, your sorrow, or your joy. Instead, they'll offer you space to feel it all—and to respond without losing yourself in the storm.

Here's what you'll explore:

- **Seeing Emotions with Zen Eyes**: How to meet each feeling like a visitor—welcome, observed, and allowed to leave
- **Teaching Stories to Tame the Inner Weather**: Tales of fire and stillness, of confusion and clarity, of pause and power
- **Practices for the Heart in Motion**: Simple, grounding tools to help you return to the breath, the body, and the moment

So now, take your seat—not above the storm, not beneath it, but within the calm at its center.

You don't have to stop the wave. You only have to remember:

You are not the wave. You are the ocean.

Let us begin again.

Chapter 13: The Ember in the Robe

Anger creates harm; anger upsets the mind. That person doesn't recognize the danger that arises within.

-The Buddha [17]

In a quiet village at the foot of a green mountain, there lived a monk named Kaito. People admired Kaito for his fine manners, his calm demeanor, and the way he always bowed low to greet even the humblest villager.

But one season, drought struck the valley. Wells dried up, rice withered in the paddies, and tempers began to flare.

One afternoon, a merchant came to the monastery to accuse Kaito:

"You monks are hoarding water!" he shouted. "You sit here, chanting, while our children thirst!"

Though the accusation was untrue, a hot wind of anger rose in Kaito's chest.

"Go out now!" he snapped. "Take your poisonous tongue elsewhere!"

The merchant turned pale and left without another word.

Kaito returned to the meditation hall, but he could not sit still. His mind replayed the argument again and again, until his stomach churned and his chest felt heavy.

That night, he couldn't sleep. His fine straw mat might as well have been a bed of thorns.

In the morning, the abbot found him pacing, face drawn tight.

"Kaito," he asked gently, "why do you look so unwell?"

Kaito confessed, "Anger came over me. It felt so justified. But now…I feel uglier than I ever have."

The abbot nodded. "Anger is like carrying a hot ember in your robe, convinced you will throw it at another. But it burns you first. Have you noticed?"

Kaito lowered his eyes. "I have. And I see how it has scorched my peace."

Together, they sat in the dawn light. The abbot spoke:

"When the ember of anger flares up, seven misfortunes follow: beauty is lost, sleep is lost, contentment is lost, wealth and respect are lost, friends are lost, and in the end, even the life you treasure can be lost."

Kaito felt the words sink in. He closed his eyes, breathing slowly. The ember was still there, but no longer blazing. He knew that next time anger arose, he would see it clearly, before it could consume him.

And so, as the sun crested the mountain, Kaito bowed to his teacher, grateful for a lesson he would never forget.

Reflection

Anger is so convincing in the moment. It insists that it is righteous, that it will fix what feels wrong. But as the story of Kaito shows, anger is an ember you clutch to throw at someone else, only to burn your own hand.

We often believe that anger will make us stronger or more respected. Yet it corrodes beauty, peace, and friendship. It drives away trust. It leaves us restless and ashamed.

In Zen, seeing anger clearly is a step to letting it go. When you recognize it—without blaming yourself or others—you have a chance to set the ember down before it does harm.

Pause today and ask yourself:

- When did anger last feel justified in my heart? What was I protecting?
- How did it affect my body, my sleep, my sense of connection?
- If I could have paused and seen it as just a passing ember, what might have changed?

Real-Life Application Scenario

Scenario: Driving in heavy traffic when you're already late

You're in the car, stuck in traffic on your way to an important meeting. Every lane seems to be crawling. You check the clock—late again. A driver suddenly cuts you off without signaling. Another car behind you starts honking. Your chest tightens and your thoughts flare up: They're so rude. This always happens to me.

You feel anger rising, like heat spreading through your body.

Then you remember the story of Kaito and the ember that burned his robe. You take a deep breath and pause.

You think, "This anger isn't going to help me get there any faster."
Instead of leaning on the horn or glaring, you slowly release your grip on the wheel. You look ahead and remind yourself that everyone here is trying to get somewhere, just like you.
Nothing about the traffic changes, but your mind settles. When you arrive, you're able to step out of the car without carrying all that tension.
You realize later that while anger was an option in that moment, it was never your obligation to pick it up.

Exploring the Quote

This quote highlights the concealed damage caused by anger.
It begins with "Anger creates harm," indicating that when anger takes control, it often spills out through words and actions that wound ourselves and others.
"Anger upsets the mind." Even if nothing is said or done, it shakes the heart, stealing peace and clarity.
"That person doesn't recognize the danger that arises within." Often, anger feels justified, but we don't see how it burns us from the inside.
In simple terms, anger is like holding a hot ember. The sooner you set it down, the freer you become.

Chapter 14: The Archer and the Crow

If one wrongs a person who should not be wronged, one who is pure and is free from moral defilements, viz., an arahat, the evil falls back upon that fool, like fine dust thrown against the wind.

-The Buddha [26]

Residing near a quiet forest, there was an archer named Daigo. Though his aim was famous across the land, so was his foul temper.

One crisp morning, Daigo prepared for a contest. He tied his hair back, strung his bow, and marched down the forest trail toward the tournament grounds.

Along the path, he saw an old Zen nun sitting beneath a cypress tree. She was chanting softly, eyes half closed, a bundle of wildflowers in her lap.

Daigo scowled. "Move along," he barked. "Your muttering spoils my focus."

The nun didn't move. She simply placed a flower on the trail in front of her.

Annoyed, Daigo drew an arrow and aimed it at a black crow perched above the nun's head. "If I cannot have my prize, at least I can prove my skill," he muttered.

He released the arrow. But just as it flew, the crow took wing. The arrow struck the branch. Startled by the noise, Daigo's horse reared, knocking him backward onto the hard stones. His head struck the path, and the world spun into darkness.

When he awoke, the old nun was pressing a damp cloth to his forehead.

He groaned, ashamed. "Why did you help me?"

"Because," she said, voice calm as falling petals, "I have no wish to see anyone harmed by their own unkindness."

Daigo closed his eyes, feeling tears gather. In that stillness, he understood at last: the sharpest arrow he had ever loosed was the one he aimed with anger.

Reflection

Sometimes, we imagine that anger will prove our strength or defend our pride. But in truth, anger blinds us. It turns skill into carelessness and confidence into harm.

Daigo's story reminds us that even when our cause feels justified, the mind clouded by irritation strikes out in ways we cannot control. In the end, the harm often lands closer to ourselves than to anyone else.

When you pause and set down the bow of anger, you discover a deeper clarity—a place where kindness and discernment grow side by side.

Letting go of anger doesn't mean you stop caring about fairness or truth. It means you care enough not to destroy yourself to prove a point.

Pause today and ask yourself:

- What anger have I carried that is costing me more than it protects?
- Who or what do I blame for my frustration? How might I respond instead with steadiness?
- What would my next choice look like if I laid down the need to strike back?

Real-Life Application Example

Scenario: During a Heated Argument at Home

Imagine you come home after a long day and discover that your partner forgot to do something important—perhaps paying a bill or calling someone on your behalf.

A spark of annoyance ignites into anger. You feel the urge to shout, to prove you are right.

But in that moment, you remember Daigo's story.

You take a slow breath and set down your metaphorical bow.

Instead of reacting immediately, you step outside for fresh air or sip a glass of water.

When you return, your voice is calmer. You explain how you feel without accusation. You listen without interruption.

Later, as you see the relief in your partner's eyes, you realize the cost you avoided by pausing: the regret of wounding someone you love just to release your frustration.

And in that quiet space, you feel stronger—not because you unleashed your anger, but because you didn't let it steer your hand.

Exploring the Quote

This quote explains why attacking a truly good person is pointless.

It begins with *"If one wrongs a person who should not be wronged, one who is pure and is free from moral defilements."* This means someone who lives with honesty, kindness, and a clear conscience—someone who does not harm others in thought, word, or deed. An Arahat or Arahant is a fully awakened being, free of greed, hatred, and delusion.

"The evil falls back upon that fool." When a person tries to hurt or slander such a good-hearted person, their hostility does not stick. Instead, it returns to the one who created it, bringing trouble and regret.

"Like fine dust thrown against the wind." If you toss dust into the wind, it blows back into your own face. In the same way, spiteful actions against a truly blameless person harm only the attacker.

In simple terms, attacking someone who lives with integrity only ends up wounding your own heart. Goodness is like the open sky—hatred cannot touch it.

Chapter 15: The Story of the Potter and the Clay

Take delight in mindfulness, guard your mind well. As an elephant stuck in mire pulls itself out, so also, pull yourself out of the mire of moral defilements.

-The Buddha [38]

In a valley of misty mornings, there lived an old potter named Anzu. When she was young, her hands shaped the finest vessels in the province—bowls so smooth and strong they were said to sing when tapped.

Years passed. Her fingers stiffened, her eyesight dimmed. One autumn, she began a tall water jar, but halfway through, her tired hands slipped. The clay collapsed into a shapeless slump on her wheel.

She sighed. A crowd had gathered to watch the famous potter, and now she felt only shame. "Perhaps," she whispered to herself, "I am too old to lift this clay."

At that moment, a young apprentice stepped forward. He had often admired Anzu but never dared speak. Bowing low, he said, "Teacher, would you show me how you began this jar?"

Anzu blinked. No one had asked her to *teach* before—only to *perform*. Slowly, she placed her hands back on the clay. Her palms remembered the centering, the steady pull. She began again, this time explaining each movement aloud.

With every word, the clay rose. With every breath, her confidence returned. By evening, the tall jar stood complete. The apprentice watched, wide-eyed.

Anzu looked at her hands, crusted in earth, and felt something she hadn't in years—gratitude for the work itself. She realized that though age had changed her body, her spirit was still the same as the girl who first pressed her fingers into the wet clay.

And when the jar was fired and placed in the village well, she touched its rim and said softly, "No matter how heavy life becomes, there is always a way to rise again."

Reflection

Sometimes, we feel stuck—trapped in the heaviness of our own fatigue, doubts, or changing circumstances. Like Anzu, we forget that strength does not always look the same as it once did.

Her story reminds us that renewal is possible, not because we force ourselves to be who we were, but because we open ourselves to *who we are now.*

When you return to the heart of what you love—not for praise or perfection, but simply for the doing—you find a hidden wellspring of energy. And in that remembering, you rise.

Pause today and ask yourself:

- Where in my life do I feel stuck or defeated?
- What might happen if I approach this place with curiosity instead of judgment?
- What simple action could I take to reconnect with my purpose?

Real-Life Application Example

Scenario: Returning to an Old Skill After a Long Break

Imagine you loved painting when you were young. But life became busy, and years passed without a single brushstroke.

One day, you open an old box of supplies. As you lift out the paints, you feel a pang of doubt— "I've forgotten how to do this."

But instead of turning away, you lay out the paper. You let your hand move slowly. You remember how it feels to mix colors, to watch them bloom on the page.

At first, your lines are shaky. But as you keep going, something inside you warms.

In that moment, you see that it doesn't matter how long it has been. It doesn't matter if your skill is rusty. What matters is that you showed up, willing to try again.

And just like Anzu, you find yourself rising, not by force, but by the quiet courage to begin.

Exploring the Quote

This quote describes the power of mindfulness to free the heart.

It begins with *"Take delight in mindfulness, guard your mind well."* Find joy in being present and aware. Protect your thoughts with care, as you would a precious garden.

"As an elephant stuck in mire pulls itself out." Even something large and strong can get trapped in mud. But with steady effort, it can rise again.

"So also, pull yourself out of the mire of moral defilements." In the same way, use mindfulness and effort to free yourself from greed, anger, and confusion.

In simple terms, stay watchful and patient. No matter how deep the mire, you have the strength to lift yourself into clarity.

Chapter 16: The Tale of Five Visitors in the Tea Garden

How is a person impulsive? It's when a certain person is fickle in faith, devotion, fondness, and confidence.

-The Buddha [10]

In a tranquil village situated among bamboo-covered hills, there resided an elderly tea master named Genshu. His garden was renowned for its serene beauty and the profound wisdom he infused into every cup of tea. People came not just for the tea, but for the way they left feeling… lighter.

One spring morning, five visitors arrived.

The first came with grand offerings—fine tea leaves, golden cups, and fragrant cakes. "For your humble tea house," he said. But after the tea was poured, he whispered to the others, "He should be grateful I came at all."

Genshu simply bowed and said, "The gift is light. But the shadow you carry makes it heavy."

The second had lived in the village for years, once sharing many meals and seasons with Genshu. Yet now he scoffed at the master's simplicity. "Still pouring tea as though it's sacred?"

Genshu smiled, "Yes, and still watching how fast yesterday's respect turns bitter in today's mouth."

The third leaned close, always with a story: "Did you hear what your disciple said about you? And what the mayor whispered?"

Genshu replied, "Words blown in the wind never reach the roots of the bamboo."

The fourth was joyful one moment, then doubtful the next. "Master, I will become your student!" he declared. Then later he said, "Your path is too silent, I'll find another."

Genshu chuckled, "Like a leaf in the stream, you chase every ripple and miss the stillness beneath."

The fifth wandered in without greeting. He stared blankly at the steam rising from his bowl. "Why do people keep talking about good or bad? It's just tea."

Genshu looked at him kindly. "When you cannot tell fire from water, it's no wonder you burn your tongue."

As the day faded, the five visitors left, each carrying their own silence.

That evening, a child asked Genshu, "Were they all wrong, master?"

He answered, "They were simply not yet ripe. We must water wisdom with patience and not drink from every passing cup."

And under the moonlight, he poured another bowl—still clear, still warm.

Reflection

We often think that wisdom only appears in great decisions or significant spiritual breakthroughs. But more often, it appears in the pauses—in how we listen, how we respond, and how we hold ourselves when others falter.

It's easy to give, then expect something in return. Easy to live beside someone, then judge them when they stumble. Easy to believe the first story we hear, to jump into moods or conclusions without staying still long enough to see clearly.

Yet Zen invites us to a gentler way. Not to rush toward judgment or away from discomfort, but to meet each moment with steadiness. To pause when we want to react. To question the stories we're fed. To choose kindness over cleverness, presence over pride.

These five reminders are not condemnations. They are mirrors—quiet ways the Dharma asks us: *Where might I be forgetting to see clearly?*

Pause today and ask yourself:

- Am I offering something with strings attached, or with genuine generosity?
- Am I listening for truth, or simply reacting to noise?
- What would it mean to stay curious rather than critical?

Real-Life Application Example

Scenario: Navigating a Conflict Among Friends or Colleagues

Imagine you're part of a group of friends, where someone has spoken critically about another behind their back. The gossip feels juicy, and it's tempting to believe it and share your own opinions. Perhaps you've helped that person generously before, but now you feel resentment building when they don't meet your expectations, making gossip feel more satisfying. In moments like this, you can recall the teachings: the one who gives and then scorns, the one who is quick to believe gossip, the one who acts on impulse. Not to judge others, but to gently turn inward and notice: *Am I doing this too?*

Instead of reacting, take a moment to breathe. You might say, "I hear your concern, but I want to understand more before forming a view," or "I gave from the heart, and I don't need anything back to validate it."

These small shifts—slowing down, questioning impulse, choosing care—build a stronger foundation than any quick reaction ever could. In this, you practice the quiet power of wise restraint and become someone others trust not for your perfection, but for your clarity, warmth, and inner steadiness.

Exploring the Quote

This teaching points to the root of impulsiveness.

It begins with *"How is a person impulsive?"* The question invites us to look not only at outer behavior, but also at what's shifting inside.

"It's when a certain person is fickle in faith, devotion, fondness, and confidence." When the heart jumps from one belief to another, from one attachment to the next, never steady, never grounded—that is impulsiveness.

It's not about how fast we move, but how unstable the mind becomes when it cannot rest in clarity.

In simple terms, impulsiveness isn't just about acting swiftly; it's when the heart lacks calm trust and keeps pursuing what seems certain for a moment but then disappears. Real steadiness comes from inner stillness, not from clinging.

Chapter 17: The Five Pebbles of Master Kaien

"When one gives birth to hatred for an individual, one should develop goodwill for that individual. Thus, the hatred for that individual should be subdued."

"When one gives birth to hatred for an individual, one should develop compassion for that individual. Thus, the hatred for that individual should be subdued.

"When one gives birth to hatred for an individual, one should develop equanimity toward that individual. Thus, the hatred for that individual should be subdued.

"When one gives birth to hatred for an individual, one should pay him no mind & pay him no attention. Thus, the hatred for that individual should be subdued.

"When one gives birth to hatred for an individual, one should direct one's thoughts to the fact of his being the product of his actions: 'This venerable one is the doer of his actions, heir to his actions, born of his actions, related by his actions, and has his actions as his arbitrator. Whatever action he does, for good or for evil, to that will he fall heir.' Thus, the hatred for that individual should be subdued."

-The Buddha [11]

At the base of Mount Haku, there lived a Zen monk named Master Kaien. Known for his unwavering calm, he was approached one day by a novice named Mio, whose face was flushed with anger.

"Master," Mio said, barely containing himself, "there's a fellow monk who mocks my efforts, interrupts my practice, and finds fault in everything I do. I've tried to be patient, but I burn with hatred every time I see him."

Master Kaien said nothing. Instead, he stood up, walked to the garden path, and returned with five smooth pebbles. He laid them gently on the mat between them.

"When you feel hatred rise," Kaien began, placing his finger on the first pebble, "offer this one—good will. Even if forced at first, breathe it in like incense. Try saying inwardly, 'May he be well.'"

He moved to the second. "If goodwill feels too far, hold this pebble—compassion. See his pain behind his actions. Remember: one who wounds is often wounded."

Touching the third, he said, "When even compassion feels strained, try this—equanimity. Step back. Be still. Neither cling nor push away."

The fourth pebble Kaien picked up and tossed aside. "Sometimes, the wise path is to give no energy to anger. No thoughts, no stories. Let him pass through your mind like wind through bamboo."

Then he held the final stone with both hands. "And if hatred still clings, remember this truth: 'He is the heir of his own actions. As am I.' This is the deepest letting go—not excusing but seeing clearly."

Mio looked at the pebbles, his breath slowing. "And what if none of this work, Master?"

Kaien smiled. "Then repeat them. The mountain yields not to one push, but many quiet winds."

Reflection

Sometimes anger feels like the only response—sharp, justified, almost righteous. But Master Kaien's five pebbles teach us another way. They show us that peace is not found by suppressing anger, but by transforming it.

Hatred, like a knot, tightens the more we pull at it. Yet the gentle hand—the one that brings goodwill, compassion, equanimity, mindful distance, or karmic clarity—can loosen it with grace.

Each person who stirs your heart in difficulty becomes a quiet teacher. They reveal where your inner stillness falters—and where it can grow. There is no need to select all five pebbles at once, if it's not possible. Just hold one. Walk gently. Let the hatred dissolve like morning mist in sunlight.

Pause today and ask yourself:

- Can I meet this tension with a wish for peace rather than punishment?
- What might this person's behavior be hiding—what wound, what fear?
- Is it possible to simply let this moment pass without fueling it?
- Might I turn my attention away, not in denial, but in care for my own clarity?
- Can I recall that each of us walks with our own karma? I don't need to carry theirs.

Real-Life Application Example

Scenario: A Family Member Who Constantly Criticizes You

You might have a relative—perhaps a parent, sibling, or elder—who seems to never stop judging you. Every visit or call leaves you drained, angry, or defensive. They don't seem to listen, and they never seem satisfied.

Try this five-step practice, like Master Kaien's pebbles:

1. **Goodwill:** Before the next interaction, pause and silently say, "May you be at ease. May I remain kind." This sets the tone within you, even if they never change.
2. **Compassion:** Ask, "What pain might live beneath their words?" Perhaps they are fearful, lonely, or repeating what they once endured.
3. **Equanimity:** In the heat of the moment, breathe. See the pattern without stepping into it. Let their words pass like clouds—not truths to hold, but weather to observe.
4. **Non-Attention:** If the conversation turns toxic, gently redirect or excuse yourself. You're not ignoring them—you're protecting your clarity.
5. **Karmic Understanding:** Remind yourself, "They will inherit their actions. I will inherit mine." You don't have to fix or fight them. Just walk your path with integrity.

Over time, you may notice less tension, fewer reactive spirals, and more space in your heart. You might even come to feel a kind of quiet gratitude—for they showed you how strong your inner peace can become.

Exploring the Quote

This teaching offers five wise ways to transform hatred when it arises in the heart.

It begins with *"When one gives birth to hatred for an individual, one should develop goodwill for that individual."* The first response is loving-kindness—consciously wishing the other person well. Even if the heart resists, this practice begins to loosen the grip of anger.

"One should develop compassion for that individual." Look deeper. See that this person, like you, suffers. Recognizing their pain allows the walls of aversion to soften.

"One should develop equanimity toward that individual." Step back and rest the heart in balance. Neither drawn in nor pushed away—just quietly aware, letting things be as they are.

"One should pay him no mind and pay him no attention." When needed, gently withdraw. Not from coldness, but from wisdom. Sometimes silence and distance are the kindest responses.

"One should reflect: this person is the owner of their actions." Each being carries the weight and result of their own karma. Understanding this dissolves the need for blame.

In simple terms, these five methods are like five gentle streams, all flowing toward the same source: a heart free from hatred. By training in these responses, we slowly release the urge to divide the world into "me and them." The mind expands, the walls fall away, and compassion becomes boundless—not just for one person, but for all.

Chapter 18: The Two Letters

If others abuse, attack, harass, and trouble you, don't make yourselves resentful, bitter, and emotionally exasperated. Or if others honor, respect, revere, or venerate you, don't make yourselves thrilled, elated, and emotionally excited.

-The Buddha [42]

In a seaside village, Master Yuma lived in a small hut beside a lighthouse. He was old, with kind eyes and slow steps, and people often came to him for advice.

One morning, a young man named Kenta arrived, visibly angry. "Master," he said, "they said terrible things about me in town—called me arrogant, lazy, and fake. I wanted to strike them!"

Yuma nodded. "Wait here."

He disappeared into his hut and returned with two envelopes. He handed one to Kenta. "Open it."

Inside was a letter that read: *You are the most compassionate, gifted soul I've ever met. The world is lucky to have you.*

Kenta blinked. "That's… nice."

"Now the second," Yuma said.

The second letter read: *You are a failure. Selfish. A fool dressed in wise words.*

Kenta frowned. "That's awful."

Yuma held up both letters. "Neither is yours."

"What do you mean?" Kenta asked.

He placed both letters into the fire.

"They are winds," he said. "If you open the window too wide to any wind, you may be blown away."

Kenta sat still for a while, then smiled.

Reflection

We often believe we need to chase praise and avoid criticism as if our worth depends on the weather of others' words. But true inner peace doesn't rise with applause or fall with insults.

In the story, Yuma taught Kenta to return, again and again, to stillness. He knew that both blame and flattery are like wind passing through a bamboo grove, making noise, but leaving no trace.

There is great strength in this kind of stillness.

When we are praised, we smile but don't cling. When we are blamed, we breathe but don't collapse. We do not hold others' opinions like treasures or daggers—we hold them like leaves. They may fall on us, but they don't define us.

Pause today and ask yourself:

- When someone praises you, do you chase more of it?
- When someone criticizes you, do you shrink into doubt?
- Can you practice the quiet courage of stillness, where neither flattery nor insult becomes your master?

Real-Life Application Example

Scenario: Navigating Praise and Criticism in Family Life

Imagine you've planned a family gathering. You've cooked, cleaned, and tried to make everything feel warm and welcoming.

One relative says, "This is wonderful—just perfect." Another mutters, "Hmm, the food could've been better last year."

Your heart tugs in two directions—part of you lights up with the praise, another part bristles at the complaint. You want to defend, explain, and prove.

But remembering Yuma's way, you pause. You smile gently at the praise, letting it land lightly like a bird resting on a branch. You hear the criticism without tightening around it. You breathe. You do not argue, and you do not shrink.

Instead, you stay present.

You look around and see laughter, full plates, people gathered—imperfect, real, alive. You realize you didn't host for approval—you hosted out of care. And that care stands untouched by either flattery or disapproval.

In that moment, you feel steady. You are not the compliments, nor the critiques. You are the kindness that held the space. And that is enough.

Exploring the Quote

This teaching provides guidance on remaining steady amidst praise and blame.

It begins with *"If others abuse, attack, harass, and trouble you, don't make yourselves resentful, bitter, and emotionally exasperated."* Painful words and actions from others are like passing storms—if you hold onto them, they weigh you down. If you let them pass, the sky clears. Responding with resentment only deepens suffering.

"Or if others honor, respect, revere, or venerate you, don't make yourselves thrilled, elated, and emotionally excited." Praise can also disturb the mind if clung to. Elation feeds ego and craving, just as blame feeds anger.

In simple terms, stay centered, whether the world lifts you up or tries to tear you down. True peace comes when your balance is not shaken by either the thorn or the flower.

Chapter 19: The Bell and the Bees

Who is a master of the ways of thought: They will think what they want to think, and they won't think what they don't want to think.

-The Buddha [41]

In Eikan Valley, a young monk named Tetsu lived in a small hermitage with a bronze bell. Each morning at dawn, he rang it once to begin his meditation.

But lately, every time he sat to meditate, a swarm of thoughts buzzed in his mind like bees. Some thoughts were sweet—dreams, plans, and praise. Others stung—old arguments, doubts, longing.

One morning, after ringing the bell, Tetsu groaned aloud, "Why can't my mind be still?"

Hearing this, old Sister Kano, who lived down the hill, came up carrying a basket of honeycombs. She listened kindly and said, "Come, help me with these bees."

Tetsu hesitated. "But I'm trying to quiet my thoughts, not gather more."

She smiled. "Then learn from the bees."

Together, they walked to the hive. As they approached, the buzzing grew louder.

"Notice," she said, "if I panic, they'll sting. But if I breathe slowly, move with care, they do not mind me."

Tetsu watched as she lifted the frame with calm hands. "The bees don't go away," she said. "I don't fight them. I work beside them. I know which to leave, which to draw close."

Back at his hut that evening, Tetsu sat again in silence.

A thought buzzed in—*I didn't train enough today.* He didn't swat it away. He noticed it, gave it no honey, and let it drift.

Reflection

Sometimes we believe the mind must be completely silent before we can rest in peace. But like Tetsu's buzzing thoughts, our minds are often filled with movement—memories, worries, desires—flitting like bees in and out of our awareness.

Stillness doesn't mean eliminating all thought. It means shifting how we relate to thought.

We don't need to swat away every distraction or force ourselves into perfect control. Instead, we learn to identify our thoughts, let them go without engaging, and softly redirect our focus back to the present, repeatedly.

Over time, we may discover that true silence arises not from suppressing the noise, but from not clinging to it.

Pause today and ask yourself:

- Which thoughts am I constantly reacting to?
- Can I let a thought come without chasing it?
- What would it feel like to be steady, even while the mind buzzes?

Real-Life Application Example

Scenario: Overthinking Before a Presentation

You're preparing for an important meeting. But your mind won't stop racing—*What if I mess up? What will they think? I should've done more.* These buzzing thoughts crowd your attention, leaving you anxious and tense.

Instead of trying to silence the mind completely, follow the beekeeper's wisdom.

Breathe.

Notice each thought as it arises—label it gently: *Worry. Planning. Fear.* Then, instead of fighting it or feeding it more attention, return to your breath or the sensation of your feet on the ground.

Say to yourself: "This is just a thought. It is not me."

When you stop trying to win the battle against your mind, you create space. In that space, steadiness grows.

And when you finally walk into the room or open your heart to speak, you'll carry the same quiet confidence Tetsu found at dawn: the peace of someone who no longer fears the bees.

Exploring the Quote

This teaching points to mastery of the mind.

It describes "*one who is a master of the ways of thought.*" This is a person who is not a prisoner of their thinking. Their mind do not run wild or turn against them.

"They will think what they want to think, and they won't think what they don't want to think." Thoughts arise, but they are not driven by them. They choose which thoughts to follow and which to let go, like a skilled rider guiding a horse.

In simple terms, this is true inner freedom. When the mind becomes your friend—not your master—you move through the world with peace, clarity, and strength.

Practice Meditation: The Garden Within

1. **Find a Still Seat.**

Sit quietly. Let the spine be upright, the body relaxed. Let your hands rest softly. Eyes closed or gently lowered. Take a few natural breaths. Allow yourself to arrive.

2. **Breathe and Anchor.**

Place your attention on the nostrils. Stay with the breath—moment to moment. Let it be natural, soft, steady.

3. **Observe Sensations as They Are.**

As you sit, sensations may arise—warmth, tightness, restlessness. Observe them clearly. Do not cling, do not push away. Note silently: *"heat... tingling... heaviness..."*—whatever arises.

4. **Allow Emotions to Appear.**

If sadness, anger, or joy arrives—pause and feel. Where do you feel it in the body? Don't analyze. Simply observe it as *a wave,* arising and passing. Note: *"sadness is here... anger is here..."* Like weather moving across the sky—let it pass.

5. **Stay with Impermanence.**

Each feeling, no matter how strong, is not permanent. Watch it change. See how it shifts, softens, or fades. Let this be your deep understanding: *"This too shall pass."*

6. **End with Compassion.**

In the final moments, place a hand over your heart. Silently offer yourself a phrase of kindness: *"I see you. I'm here. And this will pass."* Breathe once more, deeply. Then, slowly open your eyes.

Part 4: Building Emotional Resilience

Hello, Mindful Traveler,

Resilience is often misunderstood. We picture it as force, as toughness, as pushing through. But Zen reveals a quieter truth: true resilience is not about bracing against the storm—it is about *being* the still ground beneath it.

When the winds of envy, dishonesty, or self-doubt begin to howl, emotional resilience is not in how loudly you resist, but in how clearly you see.

It is built moment by moment—when you choose truth over cleverness, calm over impulse, simplicity over noise.

Like a lantern that stays lit in the wind, like a brush that moves only when the hand is steady, your strength does not have to shout. It simply *stays*—present, rooted, clear.

This part of the path invites you to build that kind of resilience. Not with armor, but with awareness. Not by tightening your grip, but by loosening what you don't need.

Here's what you'll explore:

- **Understanding Resilience as Strength**: How knowing what is false, excessive, or misaligned helps you remain grounded and responsive
- **Stories That Reflect the Strength in Simplicity**: Zen-inspired tales that reveal how integrity, patience, and quiet effort become the strongest foundations
- **Practices to Cultivate Simplicity and Resilience**: Gentle steps to protect your emotional clarity, nourish your intentions, and return to what matters most

So, are you ready to walk lighter, not because life is easier, but because *you* are clearer?

Let's begin again—softly, but with strength.

Chapter 20: The Painted Letter

For one who transgresses the Truth, and is given to lying, and who is unconcerned with the life hereafter, there is no evil that he dare not do.

-The Buddha [30]

In a lively city by the river, a talented calligrapher named Airi lived. She was famous for her graceful brushwork and the blessings she painted onto parchment. Her words hung in shops and homes, believed to bring good fortune.

But in her heart, Airi was growing restless. She envied the respect the elderly Zen master earned at the peaceful temple on the hill, as well as how everyone appreciated his calligraphy. One evening, she decided she would steal his honor for herself.

She painted a letter in her finest ink, forging the master's seal at the bottom. The message claimed the master had confessed to terrible crimes and wished to flee the temple. With careful hands, Airi slipped the letter onto the temple's altar where all could see.

At sunrise, the villagers gathered. Murmurs spread like fire. The master stepped forward and lifted the parchment in his hands. His eyes passed over each stroke.

When he looked up, he did not accuse. Instead, he said in a calm voice, "This letter is very skillfully made. The lines are balanced. The seal is precise. But the heart behind the brush—does it rest easy tonight?"

Airi, watching from the crowd, felt her face grow hot. The master set the letter down and bowed gently to the assembly.

"The truth," he continued, "is like clear water. No matter how much ink you pour into it, the water will carry the stain away. It may take time. But it always clears itself."

His gaze rested on Airi, and though he did not speak her name, she felt as if he had seen through every layer of her mind.

That evening, she climbed the hill with trembling hands and knelt at the temple door. She returned the stolen seal and said only, "Master, I wish to learn how to leave the water clear."

The old teacher nodded.

"Then begin by washing the brush."

Reflection

Sometimes, when we feel unprepared or afraid of failing, the temptation to hide the truth can feel almost irresistible. We tell ourselves it's just this once, that a small dishonesty will protect us. But every lie—even the tiniest—closes the heart and clouds the mind.
Airi's story reminds us that honesty is not just a virtue; it is a quiet, unwavering strength.
When you choose to be truthful, you may still feel nervous, but you also feel a sense of inner cleanliness. You trust yourself to stand in any light, without fear of being exposed.
Honesty doesn't guarantee success or praise. It offers something deeper: the peace of knowing you did not abandon your integrity.
Pause today and ask yourself:

- What situations make me most tempted to hide the truth?
- If I were completely honest, what burden would I no longer have to carry?
- How might my life feel if I chose sincerity, even when it's uncomfortable?

Real-Life Application Example

Scenario: During Exam Time
Imagine you're sitting in an exam hall. The clock is ticking. Your mind feels blank on one crucial question you know you should have studied. Your heart pounds.
A part of you whispers, "Just look at someone else's answer. Just this once."
But you take a breath. You feel the pull of fear, and you let it soften. You decide to stay with your own work, even if it means leaving some answers unfinished and scoring low.
When you hand in your paper, you feel uncertain about your score. But you also feel a quiet relief. You know you did not trade your honesty for a moment's advantage.
And in that moment, you learn that true confidence doesn't come from always having the right answer—it comes from knowing you did what was right.

Exploring the Quote

This quote highlights the risk of forsaking truthfulness.

It begins with *"For one who transgresses the Truth, and is given to lying."* When honesty is repeatedly broken, the mind loses its anchor.

"And who is unconcerned with the life hereafter." Without care for consequences or meaning, restraint fades away.

"There is no evil that he dare not do." Without truth and conscience to guide them, any harmful action can seem acceptable. There is no inner boundary to hold them back.

In simple terms, when lying becomes a habit and respect for consequences disappears, the heart grows careless, and harm easily follows.

Chapter 21: The Lantern and the Hot Oil

Conquer the angry one by not getting angry (i.e., by loving-kindness); conquer the wicked by goodness; conquer the stingy by generosity, and the liar by speaking the truth.

-The Buddha [31]

In a quiet Zen village by the sea, a woman named Aiko lived. She ran a small teahouse known for its warm hospitality and gentle lantern light that glowed through the evenings.

One year, a great festival was announced. People flocked to the village from faraway towns, and Aiko's teahouse filled with guests. To help with the crowds, she hired a young woman named Mariko to assist with serving tea and arranging flowers.

For many nights, Aiko and Mariko worked side by side. However, as the festival progressed, Mariko grew restless. She watched the travelers admire Aiko's kindness, and envy began to whisper in her heart:

Why do they all praise her? Why does she get all the gratitude?

One evening, as Aiko bent over the hearth to refill the kettle, Mariko lifted a pot of hot oil. Her hands trembled with jealousy. She intended to frighten Aiko, just enough to humble her.

But before she could act, Aiko turned, her eyes calm and steady.

"Mariko," she said softly, "I don't know what pain has taken root in you, but I know it is heavy. If pouring that oil will ease your suffering, then do as you must. My heart holds nothing but gratitude that you came to help me."

Mariko froze. The pot wavered in her hands.

In that moment, something inside her cracked open. She saw how small and bitter her resentment had become. She set the pot aside and fell to her knees.

"I am so sorry," she whispered, tears falling onto the tatami. "Please forgive me."

Aiko knelt beside her and placed a gentle hand on her shoulder.

"When envy is left untended," she said, "it grows like weeds in the garden. But when we meet it with understanding, it loses its power."

The lanterns flickered softly in the rafters. And there, in the hush between them, Mariko felt a peace she had never known.

Reflection

Sometimes, the hardest thing is to recognize our own jealousy. It creeps in quietly—like a shadow in the mind—whispering that someone else's light somehow dims our own.

Aiko's story reminds us that envy doesn't have to end in bitterness. When met with calm understanding instead of blame, it often dissolves on its own.

True strength is not in proving ourselves better than others. It is in being unshaken when others are caught in their own storms.

When we respond to envy with gratitude, we step out of the cycle of resentment and into a space of compassion for others and for ourselves.

Pause today and ask yourself:

- Where in my life do I feel the sting of comparison or envy?
- How might I meet that feeling with curiosity instead of judgment?
- What would it feel like to let another's success inspire me rather than diminish me?

Real-Life Application Example

Scenario: A Colleague Receives Praise You Secretly Wished For

Imagine you've worked hard on a project, but when the day comes to share it, your colleague receives most of the recognition.

At first, you feel a pang of envy—a heat rising in your chest. You catch yourself thinking: *Why not me? Why don't they see what I contributed?*

But instead of letting that resentment take over, you pause. You acknowledge the feeling without shame. You breathe into it and remember: their success does not take away your own worth.

Later, you approach your colleague and sincerely congratulate them. You reflect on what you admire in their work.

As you do, you feel the tightness in your heart loosen. You realize that celebrating others' light does not dim yours—it helps you grow.

And in that moment, your own lantern shines a little brighter.

Exploring the Quote

This quote describes the gentle power of skillful responses.

It begins with *"Conquer the angry one by not getting angry (by loving-kindness)."* When faced with anger, respond with calm goodwill instead of reacting. This disarms conflict at the root.

"Conquer the wicked by goodness." Meeting harm with virtue weakens its force. Your goodness becomes a mirror showing a different way.

"Conquer the stingy by generosity." Give freely where others hold back. Generosity melts tightness and inspires openness.

"And the liar by speaking the truth." Honesty clears confusion and sets a steady example. Truth has a quiet strength.

In simple terms, the way to overcome negativity is not to match it but to meet it with what is noble and clear.

Chapter 22: The Drums at Dawn

The wise are controlled in deed, they are controlled in speech, they are controlled in thought. Indeed, they are perfectly self-controlled.

-The Buddha [33]

In a small Zen monastery by the river, it was tradition to greet the sunrise with the soft sound of a bamboo drum—just a single tap to mark the beginning of meditation.

One year, a group of novices arrived, eager to prove their devotion. Wishing to show their energy, they decided the single tap was too modest.

The next morning, when the sky turned pale, they carried out three large drums. As the abbot prepared to sit, the novices struck the drums with all their strength—BOOM! BOOM! BOOM!

Birds exploded from the trees in fright. The old monks looked up in alarm. The abbot opened his eyes and studied the novices.

After the echoes faded, he rose and walked to the drums.

"Tell me," he asked, "did the sunrise come more quickly because of your noise?"

The novices looked down.

"Did the mountain bow to your enthusiasm?"

They shook their heads.

The abbot touched the largest drum and said, "A heart that is restless makes even the gentlest practice into a disturbance."

He invited them to sit.

"True strength," he said, "is not measured by how loudly you can declare your devotion, but by how quietly you can embody it."

From that day on, the drums remained in the storehouse, and the novices learned to welcome the dawn with a single soft breath instead of thunder.

Reflection

Sometimes we think that if we do something louder, faster, or more forcefully, it must be better. But the story of the young novices reminds us that restraint is not weakness—it is wisdom.

A quiet mind doesn't need to announce itself to be genuine. It simply settles, like morning mist over a still pond. When we act without consideration, even well-meant efforts can disrupt harmony. But when we pause, breathe, and feel our intentions, our actions naturally become gentler and more precise.

Pause today and ask yourself:

- Where am I adding unnecessary noise to prove my worth?
- What would it feel like to do the same thing with a softer presence?
- How can I honor the moment without overpowering it?

Real-Life Application Example

Scenario: Contributing to a Group Project

Imagine you are working with a team to prepare a presentation. You feel excited and want everyone to see your commitment. So, you speak often, offer constant suggestions, and fill every pause with ideas.

At first, your team appreciates your energy. However, people soon start to appear overwhelmed as important details become lost in the process rush. Some colleagues grow quiet, hesitant to share.

Instead of pushing harder, you pause. You notice your impulse to fill the space. You take a slow breath and let yourself soften. When you speak again, you do so with clarity and intention. You listen more than you talk. And in that calm, focused space, everyone feels invited to contribute.

The result is not only more peaceful, but it is also more effective. Like a single tap of the morning drum, it is just enough.

Exploring the Quote

This quote describes the quiet strength of true wisdom.

It begins with *"The wise are controlled in deed."* Their actions are careful, harmless, and guided by understanding.

"They are controlled in speech." Their words are measured, honest, and kind, never careless or hurtful.

"They are controlled in thought." Even in the mind, they watch over intentions and keep them free of greed or anger.

"Indeed, they are perfectly self-controlled." This steady discipline in body, speech, and thought is the mark of someone fully anchored in wisdom.

In simple terms, wisdom shows itself not in talk but in the gentle mastery of how we act, speak, and think.

Chapter 23: The Three Seeds

There are these three roots of what is unskillful. Which three? Greed is a root of what is unskillful, aversion is a root of what is unskillful, delusion is a root of what is unskillful.

-The Buddha [6]

One crisp autumn morning, the Zen master Sora invited her students to the courtyard. In the center stood three small pots. She gestured for them to gather close.

"These," she said, "are the three seeds that grow tangled vines inside your heart."

In the first pot, she placed a dark seed.

"This is greed," she said. "It sprouts whenever you believe more will finally fill your emptiness."

In the second pot, she placed a red seed.

"This is aversion," she continued. "It takes root when you wish the world were different, when you push away what you do not like."

And into the third pot, she dropped a gray seed.

"This is delusion," she said softly. "It grows when you forget that everything is changing or imagine that you are separate."

The students watched as she placed each seed into their pots.

Then, without a word, Sora lifted the three pots and set them aside in a dark corner. In their place, she brought three new pots, each filled with fresh earth.

"These," she smiled, "are the seeds you can plant instead."

She held up a small, bright seed.

"Lack of greed: contentment."

Another seed, smooth and white.

"Lack of aversion: kindness."

And finally, a golden seed.

"Lack of delusion: clarity."

She carefully planted the seeds in the three pots, watered them, and positioned them in sunlight. "Water these daily," she advised. "Whenever the old vines entwine your thoughts—when you want, or hate, or forget—return to these small, resilient seeds."
Her gaze grew bright and kind.
"This is how a heart becomes unbound."

Reflection

It's easy to imagine that someone else planted weeds of suffering in our garden. But every time we cling to something, push something away, or believe our thoughts without question, we slip another seed into the soil of our own mind.
Master Sora's story reminds us that we always have the chance to plant something different. We can choose contentment instead of grasping, kindness instead of resentment, clarity instead of confusion.
This is not about pretending we never feel desire or irritation. It's about noticing those habits early, before they take over everything. Each time you recognize an unhelpful seed, you have the power to pause and plant something wiser.
Pause today and ask yourself:

- Which seed am I watering right now?
- What would it feel like to plant contentment, kindness, or clarity instead?
- What small daily habit could help me grow the qualities I want to embody?

Real-Life Application Example

Scenario: When You Feel Overwhelmed by Resentment at Work
Imagine you're at work, and a colleague has taken credit for your idea in a meeting. You feel a rush of anger, and your mind spins with plans to get back at them or prove you're right.
In that moment, you can see that a seed of aversion has been planted. Rather than feeding it with stories and revenge, you pause.
You take a slow breath and ask yourself:
What seed do I want to plant instead?

You choose kindness toward yourself, acknowledging your hurt without shame. You choose clarity—seeing the situation as it is, without exaggeration. And you choose contentment, remembering that your worth isn't defined by one meeting.

Later, you calmly set the record straight with your manager, but without the poison of bitterness.

And in that choice, you feel a small, steady freedom growing—one that no one can take away.

Exploring the Quote

This quote describes the roots of all unskillful actions and is often referred to as 'the three poisons.'

It begins with *"Greed is a root of what is unskillful."* Grasping, craving, and never feeling satisfied drive actions that harm ourselves and others.

"Aversion is a root of what is unskillful." Anger, hatred, and rejection corrupt the mind, leading to conflict and cruelty.

"Delusion is a root of what is unskillful." Confusion and ignorance make us see things wrongly, leading to choices that create more suffering.

In simple terms, these three—greed, aversion, and delusion—are like tangled roots feeding unwholesome behavior. Uprooting them brings clarity and peace.

Chapter 24: The Brush and the Flame

And what is the skillful? Avoiding killing living creatures, stealing, and sexual misconduct; avoiding speech that's false, divisive, harsh, or nonsensical; contentment, goodwill, and right view.

And what is the root of the skillful? Contentment, love, and understanding.

-The Buddha [40]

A young boy named Renji apprenticed under a master calligrapher, Master Makoto. Each morning, Renji would arrive early, sweep the floors, prepare the ink, and watch Makoto create strokes of such beauty that the villagers would say the paper seemed to breathe.

But Renji's own brushwork was always restless—his lines jagged, his letters tense.

One day, after spilling ink in frustration, Renji cried out, "Why are my strokes so ugly? I try and try!"

Makoto set down his brush and motioned for Renji to go outside.

They walked in silence until they reached a fire pit where villagers had been burning old driftwood. Ashes were scattered in the breeze and around.

Makoto knelt and drew two marks in the sand using the ashes. One was graceful. The other was crooked.

"What made this one smooth?" he asked.

"The sand was undisturbed," Renji said.

"And the other?"

Renji frowned. "You dragged your hand too fast. The wind shifted. Maybe your arm shook."

Makoto nodded. "Just as with the brush."

He placed his hand over Renji's chest. "If anger fuels your stroke, it burns. If craving leads your hand, it trembles. But if your root is calm, your line will follow."

Reflection

We often try to fix the surface—our words, our work, our results—without tending to what lies beneath. However, as Master Makoto showed Renji, our actions are rooted in something deeper: our intention, our emotional state, and the place from which we begin.

When the root is steady—when we act not out of frustration, pride, or fear, but out of clarity and quiet—our efforts reflect that steadiness. Just like ink flows cleanly from a calm hand, our choices take shape more skillfully when they're not driven by craving, anger, or confusion.

This teaching reminds us that the path to wholesome action doesn't start by forcing the outcome.

Pause today and ask yourself:

- What is fueling this action I'm about to take—peace or restlessness?
- If I could soften the roots of anger or impatience, how would that change my next step?
- Can I choose a response not for the result it promises, but for the peace it plants?

Real-Life Application Example

Scenario: Deciding Whether to Help Someone When You're Exhausted

Imagine it's the end of a long week. You're physically and emotionally drained. Just as you're settling down to rest, a close friend calls, asking for something they genuinely need, but it will cost you your only quiet evening.

Immediately, your mind starts spinning:

"I should help… but I really can't. I'm exhausted."

"If I say no, will they think I don't care?"

"If I say yes, am I betraying my own needs?"

You recall the story of Master Makoto guiding Renji—how every action should be traced to its root. You pause and look within.

If you help out of guilt or fear of rejection, the root is unskillful, even if the action looks generous. If you decline with honesty and warmth, acknowledging your limitations without shutting your friend out, the root is skillful—even if the action is a "no."

So, you pick up the phone and say:

"I love you. I'm feeling a bit exhausted today. I want to support you, but if it's not urgent, I'd like to take a moment to rest and freshen up so I can be fully present for our conversation. Or is it very urgent? Then, I am listening."

Surprisingly, your friend understands. They feel seen, not rejected. You maintained your balance and offered presence, not just performance.

This is what it means to respond with awareness—not just doing the "right" thing, but doing the kind thing, rooted in clarity.

Exploring the Quote

This teaching highlights the core of what is skillful—actions and intentions that foster peace rather than harm.

It begins with *"And what is the skillful?"* These are the choices that free the heart and do not burden others.

"Avoiding killing living creatures, stealing, and sexual misconduct." To live gently, without harming, is the ground of a clear life.

"Avoiding speech that's false, divisive, harsh, or nonsensical." Words are powerful. When used with care, they become tools of truth and connection.

"Contentment, goodwill, and right view." These qualities settle the mind and open the heart. They allow one to see clearly and walk wisely.

"And what is the root of the skillful? Contentment, love, and understanding." These are the deep roots from which all peace grows—a mind that is satisfied, a heart that loves, and an eye that sees things as they are.

In simple terms, skillfulness is not a performance—it is a quiet way of being that brings no harm and gives rise to peace, within and all around.

Chapter 25: The Lantern Keeper's Way

These four things lead to the welfare and happiness of a gentleman in this life. What four?
Accomplishment in initiative, protection, good friendship, and balanced finances.
-The Buddha [18]

One quiet morning, as mist still clung to the village roofs, Ryuu came to the lantern path. His shoulders were tight, his brow clouded.

"Master Akeno," he said, voice low, "I sit in silence each day, I chant, I study. But my house is cluttered with noise. My trade stumbles. My heart feels split between coin and calm. How does one live the Way—while holding family, work, and worry?"

Akeno looked up from the lantern he was tending. The flame inside flickered steadily. He said only, "Come. Walk with me. Help me light the lanterns. I'll speak while our hands are moving."

And so, they walked, lamp to lamp. The wick caught. The glow spread.

Akeno raised four fingers.

"First," he said, "know how to begin. Start before the sun falls. Learn your tools. Shape your day with intention. This is the initiative of right effort—the work that honors work."

He lit another.

"Second—guard what you've built. The flame is not enough. Shield it from wind and thieves. Save some warmth for winter. This is the right protection."

A third finger rose.

"Third—walk with the kind-hearted. The fire shared with good companions burns cleaner. Let their wisdom polish your own."

Another lantern flared, while Akeno reached out to his fourth finger.

He said, "Fourth—balance. Too much oil, the flame leaps wild. Too little, and it dies too soon. Spend with sense. Live simply. Let enough be enough."

They reached the final lantern. Ryuu stood still, listening not just to the words, but to the spaces between them.

"Master Akeno," he said, "do you ever feel pulled in all directions?"

Akeno smiled, eyes soft. "Only when I forget which light I'm tending."

Reflection

We often believe balance means having everything under control—finances in order, family at ease, career progressing. But real balance, like Akeno's lanterns, is not a destination. It's a practice—gentle, steady, intentional.

Life is full of tasks that call for our hands and hearts. But not all deserve equal fire. When we know where to place our light, even the busiest life can become a path of peace.

Right effort means beginning with care, not haste. Right protection honors what we've already built. Right friendship keeps our inner flame alive. The right balance allows us to give without burning out.

We don't need to abandon daily life to find the way. We just need to tend it wisely—one lantern at a time.

Pause today and ask yourself:

- Where am I trying to do everything at once—and losing the spark?
- What in my life needs gentle protection?
- Who reminds me of what matters most?
- How might I live more simply, but more fully?

Real-Life Application Example

Scenario: Managing home, work, and a personal dream

Imagine you're working a full-time job, caring for family, and hoping to start a passion project—a small bakery, a podcast, a book. But everything feels too much. You're constantly tired, juggling bills and guilt.

Then you remember Akeno's lanterns. You pause.

You begin by choosing one time each week to sit quietly and plan. No pressure to finish—just to begin. That's your first lantern: *effort with care.*

Next, you review your current resources. You set aside a small fund or safeguard what you've already earned. That's your second lantern: *protecting what's already lit.*

You connect with someone who supports your vision—not for approval, but companionship. That's your third lantern: *friendship that fuels.*

And you check where your energy leaks. You adjust—not with harsh cuts, but with small changes. That's your fourth lantern: *balance without burnout.*

Life still moves, but now it moves with you, not against you. You carry your light into the world, steady and bright. And in that glow, your quiet dream begins to rise.

Exploring the Quote

This teaching points to four qualities that bring stability and happiness in everyday life. It begins with *"Accomplishment in initiative."* This is the strength to begin—taking wise, timely action rather than waiting passively. It's the courage to engage with life.

"Protection." Safeguarding what is earned through effort—your livelihood, your values, your peace. This is not fear, but care.

"Good friendship." The company you keep shapes your path. Friends who are honest, kind, and wise uplift the heart and help keep you aligned.

"Balanced finances." Living within your means, knowing how to use resources with mindfulness—neither clinging nor squandering.

In simple terms, these four—right effort, wise care, supportive relationships, and mindful living—form a strong foundation. When practiced with clarity, they bring peace not only to the mind but to the life around it.

Practice Meditation: Sitting with Change

1. **Find Your Ground.**

Sit quietly. Let the body be steady, like a mountain. Let the breath move gently, like wind through trees. Close your eyes or lower them softly. You have arrived.

2. **Begin with the Breath.**

Feel each breath rise and fall. Inhale—know you are breathing in. Exhale—know you are breathing out. Let your breath be your anchor—soft, present, alive.

3. **Open to Sensations.**

Now feel what is here in the body. Warmth, coolness, tension, ease. Whatever arises, greet it like an old friend. *"This too belongs."*

4. **Watch the Mind's Weather.**

Let thoughts come and go like clouds. Joy, sorrow, memory, fear—see them all. No need to hold. No need to chase. Know inwardly: *"Changing... changing... like wind through flame."*

5. **Feel Impermanence with Kindness.**

Notice how everything shifts—body, feelings, thoughts. Each moment arises and falls away. Even this breath will end. And that is okay. Know inwardly: *"Its change... It is what it is."*

6. **Close with Compassion.**

Simply feel the warmth of presence.

Breathe in: **"May I be steady in the winds of life."** Breathe out: **"May all beings find peace."**

7. **Return Gently.**

Let your breath deepen. Feel your seat, your body, this moment. And when you're ready, open your eyes.

Part 5: Listening Beyond Words

Hello, Heartful Listener,

Some truths arrive spoken. Many do not.

In a world overflowing with noise, opinions, and endless explanations, the art of true listening feels almost forgotten. We rush to respond, to fix, to prove—but rarely do we pause long enough to *receive*.

Zen teaches us that listening is not about waiting for your turn to speak.

When you listen beyond words, you hear more than sounds. You notice the weight of silence, the meaning between the lines, the tone that reveals more truth than the sentence ever could. You listen not only to others, but to the quiet bell of your own heart, ringing with what feels wholesome, and what does not.

This part of the journey invites you to practice that kind of listening—listening that does not seek victory but understanding. Listening that does not grasp for certainty, but rests in clarity.

By the end, you may realize that the deepest wisdom often comes without fanfare, in the hush between syllables, in the breath before the next word.

Here's what you'll explore:

- **The Art of Deep Listening**: How to hear with presence and discernment—not just sound, but sincerity
- **Stories That Reveal Silent Truths**: Zen tales showing that the clearest answers often live in stillness, not in noise
- **Practices for Wise and Compassionate Listening**: Steps to quiet the urge to react so you can meet others—and yourself—with clarity and care

Are you ready to listen—not to win, not to argue, not to fill the space, but to truly hear what life has been whispering all along?

Let's begin again.

Chapter 26: The Bamboo Scales

He is not just if he decides a case arbitrarily; the wise man should decide after considering both what is right and what is wrong.

-The Buddha [35]

Long ago, in a mountain village, two farmers came to Zen Master Hoshin with a bitter dispute over a small plot of land.

"My grandfather planted those trees," the first insisted. "This land is part of my family."

"But I have tended this soil for decades," the second replied. "It belongs to me."

Hoshin listened without interruption. Then he said, "Bring me a length of bamboo and two smooth stones."

When the farmers returned, he laid the bamboo across a wooden bench so that it could tilt like a simple scale.

"Each of you," he said softly, "hold your stone in your hands. As you speak your truth, place it gently on the bamboo."

The first farmer stepped forward and shared the story of his ancestors, his voice trembling with pride and sadness. He placed his stone on one side of the bamboo, and it tipped toward him.

The second farmer spoke of his years of labor, his calloused hands, and the harvests he had gathered. He set his stone on the other side, and the bamboo balanced in the middle, neither side touching the bench.

Hoshin looked at them with calm eyes. "Do you see? When each story is honored sincerely, neither outweighs the other. The bamboo does not decide who is right. It simply shows that both truths have their place."

He lifted the bamboo and set it aside. "Let your hearts be like this balance—able to hold each other's words without leaning into anger or greed."

The farmers bowed, and though no ownership papers were exchanged, both men left feeling something had been resolved: the quiet recognition that fairness begins when we listen without grasping.

Reflection

Fairness does not always come from proving yourself right or forcing an outcome. Often, it arises from the willingness to hold space for many stories at once—even the ones that challenge your own.

When you stop insisting that your version is the only truth, you open the door to understanding, respect, and unexpected solutions.

Like the bamboo scale, your mind can become a place where each perspective can be placed gently—without judgment tipping you into blame or defensiveness.

Pause today and ask yourself:

- Where in my life am I clinging to being "right"?
- How might I listen more openly, without immediately weighing or rejecting what I hear?
- What would it feel like to acknowledge another person's experience without having to agree or disagree?

Real-Life Application Example

Scenario: Navigating Conflict at Work

Imagine you and a colleague disagree about how a project should be handled. You feel sure your approach is more effective; they are equally convinced theirs is. Tension rises in every meeting.

Instead of pressing harder to prove your point, you choose to pause. You invite your colleague to share their reasoning fully—without interruption—and you do the same in return.

In that space of open listening, you discover parts of their perspective you hadn't considered. Perhaps you still don't agree on everything, but the energy softens. Respect grows.

And in that moment, you realize fairness isn't about winning. It's about creating a shared understanding—one balanced enough to hold both truths without collapsing into judgment.

Exploring the Quote

This quote describes the heart of fundamental fairness and wise judgment.

It begins with *"He is not just if he decides a case arbitrarily."* Someone who makes decisions quickly, without careful thought or understanding, cannot be called fair. They are simply reacting without seeing the whole picture.

"The wise man should decide after considering both what is right and what is wrong." A truly wise person pauses. They look closely at all sides—what is helpful, what is harmful, what is true, and what is false—before concluding.

In simple terms, justice isn't about rushing to judgment. It involves calmly listening and understanding first, then making a decision.

Chapter 27: The Bell of Clear Knowing

Don't go by reports, by legends, by traditions, by scripture, by logical conjecture, by inference, by analogies, by agreement through pondering views, by probability, or by the thought, "This contemplative is our teacher." When you know for yourselves that, "These qualities are unskillful; these qualities are blameworthy; these qualities are criticized by the wise; these qualities, when adopted & carried out, lead to harm & to suffering" — then you should abandon them.'

-The Buddha [4]

In a village by the river, a festival was held annually to honor the wisdom of the teachers. Dozens of masters came to set up colorful tents. Each proclaimed their teaching was the most authentic and pure.

One teacher taught that chanting alone would lead to peace. Another claimed that strict fasting was the key. A third insisted that only costly offerings to the spirits would bring blessings. The villagers drifted from one tent to the next, growing more bewildered with every word.

At dusk, an old nun named Ema arrived carrying nothing but a small bronze bell. She did not call out or build a tent. Instead, she set the bell on a smooth stone in the square.

A curious boy approached and asked, "Venerable, what do you teach?"

Ema smiled. "I teach you to ring this bell."

He frowned. "Just that?"

"Just that."

Others gathered, eager for something simple. The old nun spoke:

"When you hear a claim— *'Only this way leads ahead'*—ring the bell inside your own chest." She tapped her heart lightly. *"Listen carefully. Does this voice stir peace or fear? Does it invite kindness or pride? Does it feel like a door opening or a chain tightening?"*

She looked around the circle.

"If you feel confused, ring the bell again. If you feel grasping, ring it again. If you feel clarity and a gentle courage, perhaps you have heard something true."

A woman asked, "But how will I know for sure?"

Ema picked up the bell and rang it. The clear tone shimmered across the square.

"When you are honest with yourself," she said, "the sound is unmistakable."

One by one, the villagers closed their eyes. Each listened for the bell within them—the bell that could never be stolen by anyone else's certainty.

That evening, many tents were left behind as the people quietly walked home, carrying only the words that rang clear in their own hearts.

Reflection

Sometimes, we look everywhere for someone to tell us exactly what is true. We run from one voice to the next, hoping that clarity will be handed to us fully formed. But each borrowed certainty can become another layer of confusion.

The bell in Ema's story reminds us that true knowledge is not imposed from the outside. It is revealed when we grow still enough to hear the quiet tone within our own heart.

You don't have to be suspicious or dismissive of every teaching. But you also don't have to swallow everything you hear. When you pause to look within—asking yourself whether it brings more peace or more attachment—you are already practicing wisdom.

Pause today and ask yourself:

- What teaching or advice have I accepted without listening to the bell in my heart?
- Is this creating spaciousness or tightening fear?
- If I trusted my own quiet knowing, what would I release—and what would I keep?

Real-Life Application Example

Scenario: Sorting Through Conflicting Advice

Imagine you've been struggling with a health issue, or perhaps a life decision—like whether to stay in a relationship, move cities, or change jobs. Friends and experts all have strong opinions: *"You must do this," "Never do that," "Only this way will work."* At first, you feel pressured to pick a side quickly, to end the uncertainty. But when you slow down, you remember that clarity cannot be rushed.

You sit quietly with each option and notice what happens inside you:

Does your breath tighten or ease?

Does your heart contract or feel gently lifted?

Does your body feel small and defended, or grounded and curious?

Even if no instant answer arises, you begin to trust that listening inward is wiser than collecting more arguments. You feel a quiet confidence that, in time, the right step will feel like a bell that rings clear—and that you will recognize the sound when it comes.

Exploring the Quote

This teaching points to the freedom of direct knowing.

It begins with *"Don't go by reports, by legends, by traditions, by scripture."* Truth is not found simply by clinging to what others say or what has been passed down.

"Don't go by logical conjecture, by inference, by analogies, by agreement through pondering views, by probability, or by the thought, 'This contemplative is our teacher.'" Even clever reasoning or respect for a teacher is not enough on its own. These can become more dust on the mirror.

"When you know for yourselves that, 'These qualities are unskillful; these qualities are blameworthy; these qualities are criticized by the wise; these qualities, when adopted and carried out, lead to harm and to suffering' — then you should abandon them." The invitation is to look deeply into your own experience. See directly whether something brings harm or peace. Let your clear seeing be your guide.

In simple terms, don't lean on hearsay or blind faith. Trust the quiet authority of your own awareness. When you see what leads to suffering, put it down. When you see what leads to freedom, walk that path.

Chapter 28: The Pot of Ink

Those who discuss when angered, dogmatic, arrogant,
following what's not the noble ones' way,
seeking to expose each other's faults,
delight in each other's misspoken word, slip, stumble, defeat.
Noble ones don't speak in that way.
-The Buddha [5]

In a modest Zen temple nestled against the mountains, two novices, Koji and Ren, were known for their fierce debates.

Every evening, they sat by the lantern, arguing about the nature of compassion, the meaning of truth, or whether their teacher's silence meant agreement or disapproval.

One night, their voices grew so heated that they woke the old caretaker, Yorin. He shuffled into the hall carrying a small pot of black ink.

"Master Yorin," Koji protested, "we were only discussing the Dharma."

Yorin set the ink down carefully on the tatami mat.

"Koji," he said, "what color is this ink?"

"Black, of course," Koji replied, frowning.

"And you, Ren?"

"Also black," Ren said.

Yorin nodded. "Now—" He dipped his brush in the ink and wrote a single character on white paper. *Heart.*

"What color is the ink now?"

"Still black," the novices chorused.

Yorin placed the brush beside them. "And does the ink care whether it writes an insult or a blessing?"

The two students looked at each other in confusion.

"This is how most discussions turn sour," Yorin said gently. "You believe you are defending the Dharma, but you are only flinging ink at one another—no matter the words, the stain is the same."

He folded the paper and tapped it against his palm.

"When you speak only to defeat or to prove, your heart becomes like this ink—dark, spreading over everything. But when you speak to understand, your heart remains clear."

The novices bowed their heads, ashamed.

"Tonight," Yorin said, smiling faintly, "wash out your brushes. Tomorrow, begin again—this time, without the need to stain the world with your certainty."

And with that, he left them in the lantern's glow, the little pot of ink glistening between them like a quiet mirror.

Reflection

Sometimes we argue not because we love the truth, but because we crave to be right. We want our view to be the last word, the strongest word—the word that proves our worth. But when we cling to being right, we stain the moment with pride, impatience, and small cruelties because we stop listening, and we stop understanding.

In the end, it doesn't matter if our opinion was correct; it matters whether our words were used with care.

Yorin's ink reminds us that the intention behind what we say leaves a deeper mark than the argument itself. Speaking with humility and curiosity is like using clear water instead of ink: nothing to cover up, nothing to defend, nothing to stain.

Pause today and ask yourself:

- Am I speaking to understand, or only to win?
- What happens if I set aside the need to be certain?
- How would this conversation change if I treated it as an opportunity to connect instead of competing?

Real-Life Application Scenario

Scenario: A Disagreement with a Colleague

Imagine you are in a meeting, and a colleague challenges your idea. You feel heat rising in your chest, the urge to interrupt and defend yourself. Your mind races to find the perfect counterargument to prove them wrong.

Before you speak, you take a quiet breath.

You remember that no matter how brilliant your points are, if they come wrapped in anger, they will leave a stain. Instead of rushing to respond, you ask calmly, "Can you help me understand why you see it that way?"

You listen—truly listen.

You discover there is a concern you hadn't noticed before. And when it's your turn to share, you speak with clarity but also with respect. The room softens. The conversation opens.

In that moment, you realize that you didn't lose anything by letting go of the need to be right. Instead, you gained trust, understanding, and a glimpse of how clear communication feels—like fresh water flowing over old stones.

Exploring the Quote

This teaching describes the difference between petty argument and noble speech.

It begins with *"Those who discuss when angered, dogmatic, arrogant."* When debate is fueled by pride and irritation, it cannot lead to clarity.

"Following what's not the noble ones' way, seeking to expose each other's faults." When the aim is to attack or humiliate, the heart becomes small and defensive.

"Delight in each other's misspoken word, slip, stumble, defeat." Finding pleasure in someone else's mistake shows the mind is caught in rivalry, not understanding.

"Noble ones don't speak in that way." The wise use words to encourage truth and kindness, not to score points or prove superiority.

In simple terms, true dialogue is not a contest. It is a meeting of hearts that values honesty over winning.

Chapter 29: The Four Ways to Answer

He knows what's worthwhile & what's not, proficient in (recognizing) both, he rejects the worthless, grasps the worthwhile.

-The Buddha [8]

In the foothills of Mount Hoshin, there was a small hall where seekers came to ask Master Koji their questions.

One morning, four visitors arrived together, each with a question heavy on their hearts.

The first stepped forward, bowing low.

"Master, is there a self that remains unchanged?"

Master Koji replied without hesitation, "No."

The second asked, "When the mind wanders in meditation, is it wrong?"

Master Koji smiled gently.

"It is only natural. What matters is noticing the wandering and returning, again and again."

The third visitor bowed and said, "Why do you sit here every day? What good does it do?"

Master Koji lifted an eyebrow. "Tell me—when you breathe, what good does it do?"

The fourth visitor stepped forward, his face earnest.

"Master, how many heavens are there, and how many hells? What creatures dwell in each realm? How long is each eon?"

Master Koji closed his eyes for a moment.

Then, with a voice like a soft wind, he said, "Some questions only multiply confusion. This one, I will leave unanswered."

The four visitors sat together in the courtyard afterwards.

One had received a clear yes or no.

One had heard an explanation.

One had been given a question in return.

And one had been met with silence.

Yet all felt lighter in their hearts. For sometimes, wisdom is not in answering everything, but in knowing **how** to answer— with honesty, discernment, and a mind that sees what truly matters.

Reflection

We often believe that every question warrants a quick response—whether it's to demonstrate our knowledge, reduce our discomfort, or satisfy the questioner asking.

However, Master Koji's story reminds us that true wisdom is not about having all the answers. It is about understanding the nature of the question itself.

Some questions call for a simple, honest reply. Some need careful explanation. Some invite us to turn the inquiry back on the questioner. And some are best met with silence.

This discernment is an act of kindness. It spares us the noise of endless opinions and guides us back to what is genuinely helpful.

Pause today and ask yourself:

- Am I rushing to answer out of habit or fear?
- What would happen if I simply paused and looked more deeply?
- What is the most compassionate way to respond?

Real-Life Application Scenario

Scenario: A Difficult Conversation with a Friend

Imagine your friend comes to you late one evening, their voice tight with frustration.

"Why don't you ever support me?" they blurt out.

"Why are you always so distant? Do you even care about me at all?"

Your first impulse might be to defend yourself, to fire back with explanations or accusations. Instead, you take a slow breath. You remember that not every question needs the same kind of reply.

You see that the first question is: *Why don't you ever support me?*

It is a question of feeling, not fact. You gently ask, "What makes you feel unsupported?"

Their second question: *Why are you always so distant?*

It might deserve a thoughtful explanation of your boundaries and your own struggles.

And the third: *Do you even care about me at all?*

It calls for a simple, direct answer: “Yes. I care very much.”

Finally, when the conversation circles into blame and old resentments, you realize this is a moment to be quiet. You sit in compassionate silence, refusing to add more fuel to the fire.

In this way, you practice the four ways of answering: directness, explanation, reflection, and wise restraint. And when you finish, you both feel more seen, more understood, and more at peace.

Exploring the Quote

This teaching comes from the Pali Canon, early Buddhist scriptures, and describes the quiet skill of discernment.

It begins with *“He knows what’s worthwhile and what’s not.”* A person with clear vision understands what leads to peace and what leads to more grasping.

“Proficient in recognizing both.” They don’t guess or rely on hearsay. They see directly, with a mind that is steady and awake.

“He rejects the worthless, grasps the worthwhile.” What does not nourish wisdom is set aside. What supports freedom and compassion is embraced.

In simple terms, the heart becomes light when you stop carrying what does not matter and hold close what truly does.

Like knowing which question to answer plainly, which to explore in depth, which to return with a question, and which to set aside, wisdom means recognizing clearly where your energy and attention belong.

Chapter 30: The Empty Teacup

Don't be led into lying,

Or get caught up in affection for form.

Completely understand conceit,

and desist from hasty conduct.

-The Buddha [51]

Tomo, a proud young monk, was known for his poetic chants and handsome robes. He moved like wind, spoke like thunder, and smiled just the right amount. Visitors admired him. Novices copied him.

One day, he sat before Master Senzō, who was pouring tea into a cup that was already full.

"Master," Tomo said with a raised brow, "you're spilling it."

Senzō kept pouring. "Yes," he said. "Like praise into a heart already swollen."

Tomo sat up straighter. "I only speak the truth."

Master Senzō stopped pouring. The tea had spilled, tracing small rivers down the sides of the cup. "Even pure tea, when poured into a full cup, becomes waste."

He set the cup between them. "You're too full, Tomo. Remember that even truth, when spoken to impress, bends into a lie."

Tomo looked at the mess. "Then what should I do?"

The master handed him an empty cup. "First, empty this. Then pour only what's needed. Only then will the tea remain tea… and truth remain truth."

"Then," Senzō smiled, "you may begin."

Reflection

We often think truth is simply about accuracy—saying what's real, what's right. But in the quiet light of wisdom, truth is more than words; it's the space from which they arise. When we speak truth to impress, to control, or to protect our image, we pour clean tea into a cup already brimming with ego. Even the purest tea, poured too hastily or into the wrong vessel, spills and is lost.

Emptying the cup means letting go of self-importance, the urge to be liked, the compulsion to be seen as "the wise one." True understanding doesn't shout, and it certainly doesn't hurry. Instead, it waits. It listens. It speaks only when the cup is empty enough to receive.

Pause today and ask yourself:

- Am I speaking to share, or to shine?
- Is there room in my cup for someone else's truth?
- Can I sit quietly until my words serve clarity, not identity?

Real-Life Application Example

Scenario: A Difficult Conversation with a Friend

Your friend shares something vulnerable—an experience, a failure, a hurt. You listen, but midway through, you feel the pull to respond with your own story, to show you understand, to appear wise.

You catch yourself. You remember the tea and the cup.

Instead of pouring your own emotions into the moment, you stay with theirs. You soften your presence. You ask a gentle question instead of offering a solution.

Later, your friend says, "Thank you… I just needed someone to hear me."

You didn't try to be the healer. You didn't try to be profound.

You simply made space. And in that space, healing unfolded.

Exploring the Quote

This teaching offers a quiet reminder to walk with care, honesty, and wisdom.

It begins with *"Don't be led into lying."* False speech clouds the heart and disconnects us from what is real. Even small lies ripple outward, unsettling both speaker and listener.

"Or get caught up in affection for form." The pull of appearances—beauty, status, possessions—can trap the mind. When we cling to the surface, we miss the stillness beneath.

"Completely understand conceit." Conceit is not just pride, but the subtle habit of comparing—better than, worse than, equal to. Letting this go brings ease.

"And desist from hasty conduct." Rushing leads to mistakes. When we pause, we act with clarity rather than impulse.

In simple terms, this is a call to slow down, speak truth, let go of image, and move with the quiet dignity of awareness. The Way is not loud—it's honest, calm, and clear.

Chapter 31: The Persimmon Tree

One should follow a man of wisdom who rebukes one for one's faults, as one would follow a guide to some buried treasure. To one who follows such a wise man, it will be an advantage and not a disadvantage.

-The Buddha [23]

A young monk named Isamu worked hard in a mountain temple but often avoided correction. When his teacher, Master Genjo, pointed out his flaws, Isamu would nod politely but secretly feel stung.

One morning, while carrying water up the hillside, he dropped a bucket and sighed in frustration.

Master Genjo, watching nearby, said gently, "You rush. Again."

Isamu frowned.

Later that day, Genjo handed him a worn map and said, "There's treasure buried in the orchard. Use this."

Isamu's eyes widened. He dug for hours until his arms ached. Finally, under a crooked persimmon tree, he found a small box.

Inside, not gold, but a note:

"True treasure lies beneath your resistance."

That evening, Isamu approached Genjo with bowed head, visibly embarrassed.

Genjo smiled and handed him a new bamboo bucket. "Then your training begins now."

Reflection

We often flinch when someone points out our faults. The ego stiffens, the mind justifies, and the heart withdraws. But hidden within honest correction is a quiet kind of love—a lantern held toward the treasure buried beneath our habits.

A wise being doesn't shame us. They mirror us. Not to mock our reflection, but to help us see clearly where dust has gathered. To be rebuked with compassion is to be handed a map. A map not to someone else's version of perfection, but to our own freedom from blindness.

The proud resist. The wise lean in. It is better to be corrected than celebrated for what is false. It is better to be shown the truth than flattered into delusion.

Pause today and ask yourself:

- Do I seek comfort more than clarity?
- Can I welcome correction as an act of kindness?
- Who in my life tells me the truth—even when it's hard to hear?

Real-Life Application Example

Scenario: Receiving Feedback from Your Child

Your teenage child, quiet for days, finally says: "Sometimes you don't really listen. You just try to fix me or explain things away. It makes me feel small."

The words land heavily. Your first impulse is to defend: *"I'm trying my best. I care. You don't see all I do!"*

But then you pause—and remember the teaching: *Follow the one who rebukes with wisdom, as you would follow a guide to buried treasure.*

You take a breath. You sit beside your child, not above them. You say, "You're right. I tend to speak more than I listen. Thank you for telling me."

That evening, you don't offer advice. You simply ask, "Want to take a walk?"

No agenda. No lesson. Just your presence.

Over time, your child opens up more, not because you have all the answers, but because you've made space for their truth. And inside that space, trust returns. Not loud or grand—but steady as a lantern. You realize: Parenting isn't about always being right. It's about being willing to grow—even when the mirror is held by the ones you're raising. That kind of listening is treasure.

And the child, too, can become a teacher.

Exploring the Quote

This teaching refers to the rare gift of honest guidance.

It begins with *"One should follow a man of wisdom who rebukes one for one's faults."* Not with resistance, but with gratitude. A wise person who speaks plainly is not trying to harm, but to awaken.

"As one would follow a guide to some buried treasure." Their words may sting, but what they reveal is priceless: insight, self-honesty, and the chance to grow.

"To one who follows such a wise man, it will be an advantage and not a disadvantage." While flattery may comfort, it doesn't challenge. True guidance may feel uncomfortable, but it leads inward, toward transformation.

And when you truly listen—not just to the words, but to the stillness behind them—you hear more than correction. You hear care. You hear clarity. You hear a mirror reflecting your own potential.

In simple terms, the one who dares to show you your blind spots is offering treasure. To receive it with humility is to walk the path with open eyes.

Practice Meditation: Hearing Beneath the Noise

1. **Take Your Seat in Stillness.**

Sit upright, relaxed, grounded. Let the hands rest like calm leaves. Gently close your eyes or keep them soft and unfocused.

2. **Return to the Body.**

Feel the contact points—feet on the floor, seat on the cushion, air on the skin. Notice how the breath rises and falls, like waves touching the shore. Just sit and feel: *"This is the body... sitting, breathing, being."*

3. **Listen Within.**

Let your awareness open like a bell. Notice any sounds—near or far, sharp or soft. Don't label or follow. Simply listen without grasping.

4. **Now, Notice Feeling Tones.**

As thoughts or sensations arise, quietly ask: *"Is this pleasant, unpleasant, or neutral?"* There's no need to fix—just feel. Pleasure, discomfort, stillness—let them come and go.

5. **See the Mind as It Is.**

Now observe the quality of the mind. Is it restless? Calm? Dull? Bright? Don't judge. Don't chase. Just know inwardly: *"Knowing... knowing... this is how the mind is now."*

6. **Rest in Awareness.**

No need to analyze or control. Simply sit, breathe, and return—again and again—to what is. You are not the noise. You are the bell beneath it.

7. **Closing Gently.**

As the breath settles, let your awareness soften. Breathe in calm. Breathe out clarity. Open your eyes slowly. The bell remains.

Part 6: Finding Freedom in Acceptance

Hello, Quiet Companion,

There comes a time when the questions fall silent. When you stop asking life to be something else. When you stop demanding perfection from yourself, from others, from the world. That stillness—that soft yielding to what is—that is the beginning of true freedom.

Freedom does not always come easily. It rarely arrives when you're pushing or grasping or resisting. Instead, it slips in gently when you stop arguing with what already exists.

In this part of the path, we learn to see clearly that:

- Complaints are often smoke rising from an inner fire of unmet expectations.
- Judgment blinds us not only to others' worth but to our own light.
- Losses, far from being failures, are simply forms returning to emptiness—the open space from which all growth begins.

Here, you will sit beside the bowl of your own life—perhaps chipped, perhaps weathered—and see what's not missing, but what's still glowing quietly within.

You'll explore:

- **Acceptance as a Living Wisdom**: How to meet this moment—not as an enemy to fix, but as a teacher to receive.
- **Stories That Reveal the Peace**: Parables of fault-finding minds, broken pottery, changing tides, and bamboo's stillness.
- **Practices to Welcome Life As It Is**: Reflections and mindful steps to loosen the grip of control, soften reactivity, and honor impermanence.

Acceptance, in the end, is not giving up—it's giving space. It's the moment you stop holding your breath, and life breathes through you again.

Are you ready to stop striving, just for a while? Then come and embrace the expansive freedom that unfolds once you truly permit yourself to be present here.

Exactly as you are.

Chapter 32: The Tale of the Complaining Visitors

Blaming others is not something new. There is no one in this world who is never blamed; people would blame even a king or even a Buddha. To be blamed or to be praised by a fool is of no consequence; one is truly blamed only when he is blamed by a wise man and truly praised only when praised by a wise man.

-The Buddha [32]

In a quiet Zen temple nestled high on a green hill, there was a group of villagers who longed for wisdom. One morning, they climbed the winding path to seek counsel from the old Zen master.

The first monk they met was Elder Roku. He was known for his silence—like a great pine unmoved by any wind. When the villagers asked him questions, he simply bowed and closed his eyes.

Disappointed, they left, muttering, "He thinks he's too important to speak to us!"

Next, they found Sister Chie, a learned nun. She welcomed them warmly and spoke at length, sharing deep teachings about emptiness and form, cause and effect. But her words were like an ocean—vast, overwhelming.

They left her, grumbling, "She talks too much—who could ever understand all that?"

Still determined, they went to Brother Yuto. His teaching was like a single clear bell: "When you are tired, rest. When you are hungry, eat." Nothing more.

"That's it?" the villagers scoffed. "Too simple. He must not know much!"

Finally, they reached the Zen master. Together they complained:

"The first monk was too silent, the second too long-winded, the third too brief. No one here satisfies us."

The Zen master looked at them kindly.

"When a songbird sings, some say it is too shrill. When a mountain stream rushes, some say it is too loud. When a bell tolls, some say it is too soft. No matter what form wisdom takes, the fault-finding mind will never be at peace."

He paused, then added: "If you wish to learn, first empty your cup of complaints."

And in that moment, a hush settled over the villagers, as if the hill itself had grown still, inviting them to listen, finally, with open hearts.

Reflection

Sometimes, the mind rushes to find fault with everything it encounters. Too long, too short. Too simple, too complex. Nothing ever quite measures up.

The villagers' story reminds us that this habit of comparing and criticizing is like a restless wind—it never lets us settle. When we expect teachings, people, or experiences to match our preferences perfectly, we forget the deeper truth: wisdom is not always convenient or comfortable. It is simply what is needed.

The real obstacle is not the silence, nor the abundance of words, nor the brevity—it is the unwillingness to receive what is given with humility.

Pause today and ask yourself:

- When do I catch myself rejecting something just because it doesn't suit my taste?
- What would it feel like to meet each experience with curiosity rather than judgment?
- How might I listen more openly, trusting that there is value even when I don't immediately recognize it?

Real-Life Application Example

Scenario: Receiving Feedback at Work

Imagine you've spent weeks preparing a presentation. When you finally share it, you get three kinds of feedback:

One colleague stays silent, offering no reaction at all. Another provides a detailed critique, pointing out every flaw. A third simply says, "Good job," without any specifics.

Your mind wants to complain— "Too cold, too harsh, too vague."

But if you take a breath and set aside the urge to criticize, you may find that each response has something to offer. The silence could be an invitation to reflect on your own work without relying on approval. The critique could help you grow sharper and more prepared. The brief praise could be a simple encouragement to keep going.

When you stop rejecting and start receiving, you discover that life is always offering you the lesson you most need—if only you are willing to listen.

Exploring the Quote

This quote describes the nature of blame and praise.

It begins with *"Blaming others is not something new."* Criticism has always been part of human life.

"There is no one in this world who is never blamed; people would blame even a king or even a Buddha." No matter how virtuous, powerful, or wise you are, some will still find fault.

"To be blamed or to be praised by a fool is of no consequence." The opinions of those who lack understanding carry no real weight.

"One is truly blamed only when he is blamed by a wise man and truly praised only when praised by a wise man." What matters is the opinion of those with discernment—people who see clearly and speak honestly.

In simple terms, don't be shaken by every opinion. Trust the judgment of the wise and let the rest pass like the wind.

Chapter 33: The Lantern of a Simple Heart

It is easy to see the faults of others, but difficult to see one's own.

-The Buddha [34]

In a mountain village, there was a young woman named Lian who sold handmade lanterns in the marketplace. Her lanterns were bright and beautiful, but some people whispered that her designs were too plain or her colors too dull. Others insisted she was only trying to earn fame by copying old styles.

Each morning, Lian swept the dust from her stall and smiled at every passerby, even when they frowned at her work. She did not argue or boast.

One day, a traveling monk arrived in the village. He saw Lian sitting quietly behind her lanterns, mending a torn paper shade. He asked, "Do you mind that so many speak against you?"

Lian looked up in surprise, then stood and bowed. "Oh, I used to mind. I thought their words defined me. But then I realized that my lantern's light doesn't flicker because someone likes it or not. It shines because I tend it with care."

The monk nodded. "Would you share a lantern with me?"

She gave him her simplest one—plain rice paper, nothing more. That night, he placed it in the center of the temple hall. Its gentle glow lit the faces of everyone gathered, warming the room.

Many who had once mocked her lanterns sat in stillness, humbled by the quiet beauty they had failed to see.

From then on, Lian sold many lanterns, but she remained the same—calm, unshaken, tending her light.

Reflection

Sometimes, it is so easy to let others' judgments become the measure of our worth. We believe their praise proves our goodness, and their criticism proves our failure. But like Lian's lantern, our true light is not fueled by opinions—it is kindled by sincerity. When we tend our craft, our relationships, or our own heart with honesty and patience, we discover a steady glow that no passing comment can dim.

Acceptance does not mean we agree with every opinion or approve of every outcome. It simply means we stop struggling against what we cannot control and allow ourselves to see things as they really are.

When we relax our grip and allow reality to be reality, we find the spaciousness to respond with wisdom instead of reactivity.

Pause today and ask yourself:

- What am I mainly doing to please others, rather than from my own conviction?
- How do I react when someone misunderstands or criticizes me?
- What would it feel like to simply keep tending my lantern without needing it to be admired?

Real-Life Application Example

Scenario: Sharing Your Work in Public

Imagine you've poured your heart into a project—a painting, a report, or a community event. The moment comes to share it, and you hear a few voices whisper that it isn't impressive, or that you should have done it differently.

At first, you feel a wave of self-doubt. Maybe they're right. Maybe you should hide your work or prove yourself.

But then you remember Lian's lantern: you created this because you cared, because it mattered to you. You take a slow breath and thank them for their thoughts without defending or explaining.

Later, someone quietly tells you your project made a difference to them—that it brought them hope or inspiration. And in that moment, you feel a quiet confidence that grows not from praise, but from knowing you stayed true to your own light.

Exploring the Quote

This quote describes the common habit of looking outward instead of inward.

It begins with *"It is easy to see the faults of others."* The mind quickly notices what others do wrong, pointing out their flaws and mistakes.

"But difficult to see one's own." Turning that same honest gaze toward ourselves takes humility and courage.

In simple terms, it is simpler to judge than to reflect. Real growth begins when we look clearly at our own hearts and accept others as it is.

Chapter 34: The Potter's Bowl

And so, they regard it as empty of what is not there, but as to what remains, they understand that it is present.
-The Buddha [43]

In a small mountain village, a humble potter named Taiga lived. Every morning, before shaping his clay, Taiga would walk up the hill to visit the old Zen teacher, Master Minato.

One dawn, Taiga arrived carrying a cracked bowl in both hands. He set it before Master Minato and bowed deeply.

"Master," he said, "this was my best work. I fired it carefully and polished it until it shone. But it slipped from my hands. Now it is broken, and I feel empty inside."

Master Minato studied the bowl for a long while. Then he picked it up gently and turned it over in his palms.

"Taiga," he began softly, "tell me: when this bowl was whole, what did you see in it?"

"I saw something perfect," Taiga said. "A vessel I had shaped with all my skill."

"And now?" the master asked.

"Now I see what is missing," Taiga whispered.

Master Minato nodded. He set the cracked bowl between them and tapped it lightly with a wooden stick. The soft, hollow sound echoed in the morning air.

"This emptiness," he said, "was here all along. Even when the bowl was unbroken, it was empty of water, empty of rice, empty of flowers. Its emptiness is what made it useful."

He looked up at Taiga, his eyes kind.

Taiga felt his breath deepen. The morning breeze touched his face, and he understood.

"The crack in this bowl," Master Minato continued, "does not destroy its emptiness. It only reveals it more clearly. When you see the true nature of all things—empty of any fixed self—you no longer cling to the shape they once held."

He placed the bowl back into Taiga's hands.

"Go," he said, "and make another. But do not forget that what you call emptiness is never a loss. It is the space in which everything begins."
Taiga bowed again and walked back to his workshop, gently holding the broken bowl in his arms.

Reflection

Sometimes, when something dear to us breaks—a project, a relationship, an idea of who we thought we were—it feels like a failure. Like Taiga holding his cracked bowl, we see only what is missing.
Yet when we look more closely, we discover that the emptiness we fear is not an absence, but a quiet, spacious possibility. It is the openness that was always there, hidden beneath our certainty and attachment.
Emptiness doesn't mean nothing matters. It means nothing is fixed or final. The forms we cherish arise and pass away, but the clear space that holds them is never destroyed. You see that cracks are not the end of usefulness—they are an invitation to begin again with new understanding.
Pause for a moment and ask yourself:

- What am I clinging to so tightly that I can no longer see the open space around it?
- What might become possible if I stopped grasping for wholeness and allowed things to be as they are, incomplete?
- What hidden freedom might be waiting inside this very emptiness?

Real-Life Application Scenario

Scenario: Letting Go of a Project That Didn't Work Out
Imagine you spent months pouring your heart into a creative project—a new business idea, a community event, a book. You believed it would be your finest work. However, despite your efforts, it didn't unfold as you had hoped.
At first, you feel hollow, as if all your skill and care were wasted.

But instead of rushing to fill that emptiness, you pause. You sit quietly with the disappointment. Like Taiga, you turn the broken shape over in your hands and see it clearly. Gradually, you realize that this emptiness is not a void to fear—it is space to grow. Because nothing is set in stone, you can start again. You can take what you learned—your discipline, your insight, your resilience—and create something new.

The next time you start shaping your clay, you do it with less grasping and more openness. You understand that every form is temporary, and in that understanding, you find a deeper peace that no success or failure can take away.

Exploring the Quote

This teaching describes the gentle precision of clear understanding.

It begins with *"And so, they regard it as empty of what is not there."* When looking closely, you see that many things you imagined—fixed ideas, identities, stories—are simply not present.

"But as to what remains, they understand that it is present." What is actually here—this moment's experience, this body, this feeling—is seen just as it is, without adding or subtracting.

In simple terms, wisdom is knowing what is empty and what is real, resting in the simplicity of what remains.

Chapter 35: The Five Pebbles

All beings are the owner(s) of their actions, heir(s) to their actions, born of their actions, related through their actions, and have their actions as their arbitrator. Whatever they do, for good or for evil, to that will they fall heir.

-The Buddha [9]

In a quiet village near the sea, there lived Kenzo, an old gardener known for his calm presence. Each morning, he would climb the cliffs carrying a small basket filled with pebbles he had gathered over many years.

One day, a young potter named Aoto followed him, curious to learn why the old man seemed so at peace. Kenzo sat down on a sun-warmed boulder, set the basket between them, and selected the first pebble—a gray stone veined with white lines.

“See this one?” he asked. “Its cracks grew deeper each season, though it never broke. It reminds me that time leaves its mark on us all. We age, but we remain.”

He set it aside and chose a second pebble, pitted and rough from countless tides.

“This one was once smooth as glass. Illness and hardship can weather us just the same.”

Next, he lifted a bright stone flecked with bits of green.

“This pebble once belonged to a cliff far away. The sea carried it here. Just as life moves us from place to place.”

He placed a pale, perfectly round pebble in Aoto’s hand.

“This one looks unchanging,” Kenzo said, “but inside it is full of tiny fractures you cannot see. One day it may split. Everything we treasure, everything that seems solid, will eventually transform.”

Finally, he picked up the smallest stone, dark and heavy.

“This pebble I found deep in the sea. It reminds me that my actions—good or bad—stay with me and have a lasting impact. No tide can wash them away.”

Aoto turned each stone in his palm, feeling their weight, their scars, their hidden cracks.

“Does knowing this make you sad?” he asked.

Kenzo's eyes softened.

"No," he replied. "It helps me live honestly. When I remember how all things change, I care less about clinging and more about appreciating small acts of kindness and making the most of each moment."

The two of them sat quietly, watching the waves. Aoto felt something loosen in his heart—a tenderness for the world as it is.

Reflection

Sometimes we think stability is something we can build and keep forever, like a tower of stones that will never fall. But life is more like Kenzo's basket of pebbles: each one shaped by scenarios we cannot command.

Aging, uncertainty, and change are not failures—they are the simple truths of being alive. When we look closely, we see how even the cracks and rough edges belong.

This does not have to make us fearful. In fact, it can open a gentler way of seeing. If everything we love is destined to transform, then each moment is more precious, not less. Each act of care matters more, not less.

When you remember that all things are in motion, you can let go of striving to control what cannot be held and instead bring your presence fully to what is here now.

Pause today and ask yourself:

- What am I clinging to, hoping it will stay unchanged?
- What would it feel like to meet this moment without needing to hold it still?
- How might I honor both the beauty and the impermanence of all that I love?

Real-Life Application Example

Scenario: Facing Uncertainty in Relationships

Imagine you've worked hard to build a relationship that feels secure. Recently, you feel that changes are coming—whether it's a partner exploring new paths or your own priorities shifting.

At first, you might feel resistance, like clutching a pebble so tightly your hand aches. But when you remember Kenzo's basket, you can see that change is not a threat—it's the nature of things.

Instead of blaming yourself or others, you can begin to soften around the unknown. You can meet the situation with curiosity rather than fear, and ask:

How can I respond with honesty and care, even as circumstances transform?

What small kindness can I offer—to myself and those around me—right now?

In that acceptance, you discover an unexpected freedom: the strength to stay grounded while everything shifts, and the courage to begin again.

Exploring the Quote

This teaching describes the quiet truth of karma.

It begins with *"All beings are the owners of their actions, heirs to their actions."* No one can escape the fruits of what they do. Our deeds are ours alone.

"Born of their actions, related through their actions." What we choose shapes who we become and how we connect to others.

"And have their actions as their arbitrator." Our actions ultimately determine the quality of our life and mind.

"Whatever they do, for good or for evil, to that will they fall heir." Just as a field yields the seeds you plant, each action ripens in its time.

In simple terms, your life is shaped by the choices you make. Plant wisely, and you will harvest peace.

Chapter 36: The Bamboo Test

'I will be skilled in reading my own mind.'

-The Buddha [19]

Each spring, the villagers came to Master Takuma's retreat to study silence, discipline, and the ways of the mind. Among them this year was a young man named Jun, eager and proud.

Jun believed he already understood meditation well—he had read every scroll, memorized every technique, and could sit longer than anyone in the group. But still, something troubled him: a restlessness he could not name.

After the morning sitting, Master Takuma gave each student a strip of bamboo and said, "Take this home. Watch it daily. Return in seven days with what you have learned."

Jun was confused. *"It's just bamboo,"* he thought. *"What am I supposed to find?"*

Each day, he sat before the bamboo, waiting for wisdom to reveal itself. But all he saw was a green stalk, unmoving. On the sixth day, angry and tired, he snapped at a fellow student, blamed the bamboo, and nearly threw it away.

But on the seventh morning, something changed.

He noticed a single dew drop glinting on the leaf's edge. The bamboo stood still—not striving, not speaking, not comparing—just quietly growing, rooted in place.

That day, he returned to the temple. When Master Takuma asked what he saw, Jun bowed.

"I saw myself—rushing, proving, resisting. I sat beside the bamboo expecting it to change… but I was the one who needed to soften."

The master nodded. "Good. You looked at it long enough to see beyond it. Most people look everywhere but within. Few are brave enough to sit with their own shadows."

Reflection

We often believe that spiritual insight must be dramatic or that self-mastery is about force—pushing away what we dislike, pulling toward what we want. But like Jun before the bamboo, we learn that clarity does not arise from control. It blooms from stillness, from watching without grasping.

True self-awareness is not a performance. It is a quiet honesty. It's the courage to sit with your restlessness, to notice when you're rushing, comparing, or covering up discomfort.

The bamboo didn't preach. It just stood. Growing when the time was right. And so too can we, when we stop demanding revelation and begin practicing gentle presence.

Pause today and ask yourself:

- Am I watching my mind, or trying to escape it?
- What reaction within me needs softening rather than solving?
- Can I sit with my discomfort long enough to see what lies beneath it?

Real-Life Application Example

Scenario: Feeling Stuck in Personal Growth

Imagine you're in a period of self-development. You've read the books, taken the courses, practiced the affirmations—but still, there's a nagging frustration: you don't feel "better."

You may feel tempted to abandon the path, to try something louder or faster. But instead, you remember the story of Jun and the bamboo.

So, you do something simple: you sit. You take a few quiet moments each day, not to fix yourself, but to observe. You notice your impatience. You notice your inner critic. You even notice moments of peace that often slip by unnoticed.

You begin to journal—not to impress, but to reflect. You don't demand answers. You let insight come in its own time.

Weeks later, you realize something subtle has shifted. You're not reacting so quickly. You speak more gently to yourself. You listen more deeply to others. You are not rushing to be perfect.

You are simply becoming—like the bamboo—rooted, resilient, and quietly growing in your own season.

Exploring the Quote

This teaching speaks about the quiet strength of self-awareness.

It begins with *"'I will be skilled in reading my own mind.'"* One may not have deep insight into others' thoughts or feelings, and that's okay. Knowing others is helpful—but not essential on the path. What truly matters is knowing one's own heart—seeing clearly what arises, what passes, and how the mind moves.

In simple terms, don't worry about reading others. Turn the light inward. When you know your own mind deeply and honestly, wisdom begins to bloom. Peace comes not from knowing everything, but from knowing yourself well.

Chapter 37: Just This

In reference to the seen, there will be only the seen. In reference to the heard, only the heard. In reference to the sensed, only the sensed. In reference to the cognized, only the cognized. That is how you should train yourself.

-The Buddha [53]

Naoki was a restless seeker. He had sat with monks in snowy mountains, fasted with sages by the riverside, and listened to philosophers debate until night dissolved into dawn. Still, peace escaped him like mist in the morning sun.

One evening, he met an old wanderer who was polishing a wooden bowl under a tree.

"Master," Naoki asked, "where do I find the Way?"

The old man looked up, eyes gentle. "Have you eaten today?"

Naoki blinked. "Yes."

"Then go wash your bowl."

Naoki frowned. "But… I meant enlightenment."

The old man smiled, setting the bowl down. Then listen carefully, and as you wash, let only what is seen be seen, only what is heard be heard, only what is tasted be tasted, and only what is thought be thought.

Naoki tilted his head. "What does that mean?"

"When you see, do not add your name to it. When you hear, do not wrap it in stories. When you feel, do not cling to or push away. When you think, do not become your thoughts."

The wind stirred the leaves. Naoki stared at the bowl.

"No fixing. No chasing. No escaping," the old man said. "Just this."

In that moment, Naoki didn't feel separate. Not from the bowl. Not from the breath. Not even from the question.

He bowed low. "Thank you, Master…"

But the man was already gone—like a wave that left no trace.

Reflection

We often believe awakening is some distant mountain to climb, something grand to be earned after years of struggle. But the teaching whispered is quiet, immediate, and disarming: *In the seen, only the seen. In the thought, only the thought.*

Awakening is not becoming something else. It is letting go of the one who clings. We suffer not because we see or feel or think—but because we *add* ourselves into everything:

"This is my pain."

"This means I've failed."

"This must not change."

But when we simply see the seen… hear the heard… feel the felt… without naming, grabbing, resisting—there is peace. Not dull, not distant—just *spacious and simple.* In that space, there is no burden of becoming. Just the ease of being.

Pause today and ask yourself:

- Can I meet this moment without labeling it?
- What story am I adding to this experience?
- If I don't wrap this thought in "me" or "mine," what remains?

Real-Life Application Example

Scenario: Overthinking After a Difficult Conversation

You've had a tense conversation with someone you care about. Hours later, your mind keeps replaying it—looping through what was said, what wasn't, what you *should have* said. You feel tight, consumed, and unsettled.

But then you remember: *"In the heard, only the heard. In the thought, only the thought."*

You pause. Breathe.

You recognize: This is a thought. A memory. A sound in the mind.

You don't need to argue with it, fix it, or follow it. You let the thought pass like a cloud.

Then the feeling in your chest—tightness. That too… just a sensation. Not wrong. Not yours. Just here.

You gently return to now.

A cup of tea. The sound of rain. The simple warmth of the breath.

In not clinging to the past or becoming your thoughts, you rediscover the stillness that was never lost.

This, *just this*, is enough.

Exploring the Quote

This teaching offers a profound and simple instruction for resting in pure awareness.

It begins with *"In reference to the seen, there will be only the seen."* When seeing happens, just let there be seeing—no story, no judgment, no clinging.

"In reference to the heard, only the heard. In reference to the sensed, only the sensed. In reference to the cognized, only the cognized." Whether it's sound, sensation, or thought, the practice is the same: experience what arises as it is, without adding anything extra.

"That is how you should train yourself." This is a training in simplicity and presence. It's not a withdrawal from life, but a return to direct, clear seeing.

This way of being cultivates deep acceptance. When we let things be just what they are—without resistance, grasping, or aversion—we begin to soften. The heart no longer fights the moment. Peace arises, not from controlling the world, but from meeting it as it is.

In simple terms, let the moment speak for itself. When you no longer argue with what is, acceptance becomes natural—and with it, freedom.

Practice Meditation: The Space of Emptiness

1. **Take Your Seat.**

Sit upright, quietly grounded. Let your hands rest softly. Close your eyes or lower your gaze. Settle into stillness.

2. **Rest with the Breath.**

Follow the natural breath—in, out. No need to count. Just observe, gently. Let the breath arrive and leave like clouds through open sky.

3. **Reflect Gently.**

Now, whenever a thought arrives at your awareness, gently reflect:

"Everything I see, everything I feel, is only a name."

"Nothing exists on its own. It is only labeled by the mind."

"This body, this thought, this 'I'—just names, passing shadows."

Allow these reflections to resonate softly, without needing to solve or analyze them. Let them rest in your awareness like leaves on a still pond.

4. **Sit in the Vastness.**

Let all things—sounds, thoughts, even the sense of self—arise and pass, without clinging.

No ground to stand on. No object to hold.

Only awareness, wide and clear, like open sky.

5. **Return to Just This.**

When your mind wanders, return to the breath. Return to the knowing: "This too is empty."

Sit in the freedom of not needing to grasp.

6. **Close Softly.**

Breathe deeply. Bow to the quiet truth that nothing is fixed—and yet, all is deeply present.

Emptiness is not nothing. It is spaciousness. Possibility. Peace.

Part 7: Cultivating Compassion

Hello, Gentle Witness,

Compassion is not always loud. Sometimes, it's the whisper that says, "I won't fight back." Sometimes, it's a presence in the rain, a hand that holds warmth, a voice that chooses softness over sharpness.

In a world of quick judgments and worn hearts, true compassion demands something deeper than a reaction—it requires *understanding*.

This part of your journey is about learning how to care with wisdom. It's about tending wounds—yours and others'—without reopening them again and again. It's about letting go of bitterness before it takes root, speaking truth without harm, and choosing kindness not because it's easy, but because it's freeing.

Stories in this part remind us that compassion isn't always about doing more; it's about doing the right thing with greater presence. It is the choice to soften when you could harden. To pause before the sharp word. To give what is hard to give, and receive what is easy to forget: thanks, tenderness, trust.

Here's what you'll explore:

- **Understanding Compassion the Zen Way**: How care becomes a force of clarity, not exhaustion
- **Stories That Show Gentle Compassion in Action**: Tales of forgiveness, and speaking with heart
- **Practices for Compassionate Living**: Daily reflections and steps to embody kindness without losing yourself

By the end, you may find that the most radiant compassion is not the one that tries to save everything, but the one that simply *stays*, without fear, without force.

So come—light your lantern, not to burn, but to warm.

Let's continue.

Chapter 38: The Tale of the Bitter Fruits

Enmity cannot be appeased by enmity; it can only be appeased by loving-kindness.

-The Buddha [36]

Near a quiet village tucked beneath green hills, there grew a tree called the Bitter Tree. No one remembered who planted it, but everyone knew its fruit was bitter.

One summer, a farmer named Emiko found that her neighbor's goats had eaten the cabbages along her fence. Furious, she tore down the fence and let her own cattle trample the neighbor's garden in revenge.

The neighbor, seeing the ruin, waited until autumn, then slipped into Emiko's orchard at night and poured salt around the roots of her best trees.

Seasons passed. Their children grew up watching this silent feud—each harvest bringing a new act of spite. No apology was ever offered. No forgiveness was ever spoken. The Bitter Tree in the village center appeared to thrive with each act of their resentment.

One day, an old Zen teacher named Kisho came to the village. He sat beneath the Bitter Tree and watched the farmers bicker in the fields. When Emiko walked by carrying a basket of spoiled fruit, Kisho called to her gently:

"Tell me, how does this tree's fruit taste?"

"It tastes bitter," she said, frowning.

"And yet," he replied, "you keep watering it."

Emiko set down her basket, weary in body and soul. "I don't know how to stop," she admitted, as she understood what he was asking.

Kisho picked up a dry branch and traced a circle in the dust. "Every time you choose anger, you walk this circle again. If you wish to be free, you must step outside it."

Emiko looked at the circle, then at her neighbor standing nearby, arms crossed.

"It's really enough," she whispered softly.

Reflection

Sometimes, we don't realize how much energy it takes to keep old grudges alive. Like Emiko's story, resentment puts down roots in the heart, nourished by our repeated stories of injury and blame.

We think holding on will protect us or make us strong. But in truth, it only poisons our peace. Letting go of enmity is not about saying what happened was acceptable. It is about ending the cycle that keeps wounding us again and again.

When we choose to set down the weight of revenge—even a little—we make space for something fresher and kinder to grow.

Pause today and ask yourself:

- What old grudge have I been watering without realizing it?
- Who or what would I be without this bitterness?
- What small gesture could I take to step out of the circle and begin again?

Real-Life Application Example

Scenario: Tension Between Colleagues

Imagine you have a colleague who once spoke harshly to you in a meeting. You felt humiliated, and since then, you've carried that resentment.

Weeks pass, and every time you see them, your stomach tightens. You replay the moment in your mind. You don't realize how much of your energy is tangled in this silent hostility.

One day, you pause and notice: it feels heavy. You decide to stop nourishing the grudge. You don't have to pretend it didn't happen, but you choose not to keep replaying it.

You acknowledge your own hurt with honesty. Then you quietly let go of the story: "This doesn't have to define me."

The next time you cross paths, instead of turning away, you nod politely. You feel lighter. A small step, but enough to begin leaving the old circle behind.

Exploring the Quote

This quote describes the only way to truly end conflict.

It begins with *"Enmity cannot be appeased by enmity."* Hatred answered with more hatred only feeds the fire. Anger returned with anger keeps the cycle going.
"It can only be appeased by loving-kindness." When you meet hostility with goodwill and understanding, the tension begins to soften. This is how enmity dissolves.
In simple terms, fighting anger with anger is like pouring oil on flames. Only kindness has the power to bring real peace.

Chapter 39: The Bamboo and the Bell

A person who is accused should ground themselves in two things: truth and an even temper. Even if others accuse me—at the right time or the wrong time, truthfully or falsely, gently or harshly, beneficially or harmfully, lovingly or with secret hate—I will still ground myself in two things: truth and an even temper.

-The Buddha [12]

A Zen master named Eikan was known for his gentle teaching style. One morning, a novice named Ren rushed to him, eyes wide with anger.

"Master, Koji has been stealing extra rice from the kitchen. I saw it with my own eyes. Shouldn't we confront him immediately?"

Eikan was sitting beneath a tall bamboo grove, sipping hot tea. He gestured for Ren to sit and asked, "Tell me, Ren, is your voice steady? Is your heart clear?"

Ren paused. "I… I'm not sure."

Eikan pointed to the wind chime hanging from the temple bell.

"Do you see that bell?" he asked. "It rings only when struck at the right moment. Hit it too soon or too harshly, and it makes a dull sound. But with patience and the right touch, its song can wake even a sleeping valley."

Ren sat in silence.

"Koji may have his reasons," the master said softly. "If you wish to speak, make sure you ring the bell—gently, truthfully, with benefit, and from a place of care. Not to humiliate, not to shame, but to awaken."

Later that evening, Ren approached Koji—not with accusation, but with curiosity. "Is everything all right, brother? I've noticed you visiting the kitchen often."

Koji's eyes welled. "My sister sent word—our family is in debt. I've been saving my rice to send home."

Instead of punishment, the monks offered Koji help. And the temple quietly began a practice of sharing a portion of their meals each month with those in need.

Reflection

Sometimes we think the truth alone is enough. But truth, without the right moment and the right heart, can harm more than heal. In the Zen way, speech is not just about accuracy—it's about intention, timing, and tone.

Ren's story reminds us that even the clearest truth needs gentleness to land well. Like the sound of a temple bell, words resonate differently depending on how they are offered. When spoken with care, truth becomes a bridge—not a blade. It opens, rather than closes.

Correction is not a weapon. It's an invitation to return, to reflect, to begin again. And when we speak not to scold but to serve, something softens in both speaker and listener.

Pause today and ask yourself:

- Am I speaking from wisdom or from reactivity?
- Is my correction rooted in care or in frustration?
- How can I convey truth in a way that helps, rather than harms?

Real-Life Application Example

Scenario: Offering feedback to someone who made a mistake.

You notice a family member has made a misstep—perhaps they've forgotten a commitment. You feel the urge to speak up immediately.

At first, frustration may rise. But instead of reacting, you pause and breathe. You remember Ren's moment with the Zen master. Correction is most powerful when it's calm, not heated.

You choose your time. In a quiet moment, you speak—not to blame, but to understand. You share how their action affected you. You listen. You stay steady. You let compassion guide your words.

And because you do, something shifts. Defenses lower. Honesty opens. What could have turned into distance becomes a space of growth and repair.

In choosing clarity without cruelty, you become a bell—not an alarm. You remind others, gently, of what matters. This is the quiet strength of Zen speech—firm, kind, and clear.

Exploring the Quote

This teaching emphasizes the importance of inner composure.

It begins with *"A person who is accused should ground themselves in two things: truth and an even temper."* When words come at you—true or false, kind or cruel—the steady heart doesn't waver.

"Even if others accuse me—at the right time or the wrong time, truthfully or falsely, gently or harshly, beneficially or harmfully, lovingly or with secret hate..." Life offers many voices, some honest, some twisted. Praise and blame blow in like changing winds.

"I will still ground myself in two things: truth and an even temper." No matter what comes, stay rooted in what is true and keep the mind calm and compassionate, like a mountain unmoved by the storm.

In simple terms, don't be pulled by every opinion. Stand in truth, and let your calm be your shield. Always show compassion, regardless of the circumstances.

Chapter 40: The Friend in the Storm

A friend endowed with seven qualities is worth associating with. Which seven? He gives what is hard to give. He does what is hard to do. He endures what is hard to endure. He reveals his secrets to you. He keeps your secrets. When misfortunes strike, he doesn't abandon you. When you're down & out, he doesn't look down on you.

-The Buddha [15]

The rain had not stopped for five days.

Kaito sat on the creaking porch of the temple, staring into the gray curtain of water. His robe was damp. His rice jar was nearly empty. But heavier than the clouds above was the weight in his chest.

"I don't think I can do this anymore," he whispered to no one.

The gate creaked.

Through the rain walked Osamu, cloak soaked, a small bundle tucked under one arm. He stepped inside without a word, unwrapped warm rice cakes and a flask of miso, and placed them beside Kaito.

"You walked through this storm?" Kaito asked, startled.

Osamu poured the soup and handed it over. "Some paths are worth walking, even if they wash the footprints away."

They sat together, side by side, the silence between them calm, not empty.

After a while, Kaito said, "Why do you keep coming? I am of no use. No answers. No gold. Not even tea."

Osamu looked out at the rain, then back at Kaito. "But we are friends."

Kaito turned toward him and looked down at the warm rice in his hands. And for the first time in many days, something inside him softened.

That night, as the storm sang on, two friends sat in quiet companionship—no riches exchanged, no words needing proof. Just the soft presence of someone who stayed.

Reflection

We often think of friendship as a fair exchange—shared joys, mutual gain, give and take. But real friendship, like Osamu's presence in the storm, doesn't arrive with balance sheets or sunny conditions.

A true friend doesn't wait until things are convenient or comfortable. They walk through the storm—not to fix you, not to save you, but simply to sit beside you when the rest of the world walks away.

These friends give what is hard to give: time when they have none, patience when you're difficult, warmth when you're cold with doubt. They keep your secrets close, carry your burdens quietly, and never measure your worth by your usefulness.

When you feel like you've failed, they don't look down. They look *in*—and remind you of what's still whole.

Pause today and ask yourself:

- Who in your life shows up without needing anything back?
- How do you show up for others—not just when it's easy, but when it's hard?
- Can you be the friend who doesn't weigh the rain?

Real-Life Application Example

Scenario: Supporting a Friend Through a Difficult Time

Imagine your closest friend has lost their job and is pulling away. They've stopped returning messages and have gone quiet, their usual spark dimmed.

At first, you feel unsure—do they want space? Will you say the wrong thing?

But remembering Osamu, you don't wait for the rain to pass. You show up. Maybe you bring food, maybe just your presence. You say little, judge less, and stay a while.

You remind your friend they're not broken, not alone, not worthless. You don't ask them to be cheerful. You ask them to simply be, and you remain there as well, offering strength and compassion.

No grand speeches. No solutions. Just presence.

In that presence, trust grows. In that stillness, healing begins.

And when the clouds finally clear, your friend will remember—not just that they endured, but that someone stayed when they couldn't stand tall.

That is the shape of real friendship.

Exploring the Quote

This teaching describes the rare and beautiful qualities of a true friend.

It begins with *"A friend endowed with seven qualities is worth associating with."* True friendship is not found in charm or convenience, but in quiet, steady goodness.

"He gives what is hard to give." A true friend shares not only possessions but time, energy, and even their own peace of mind when you need it most.

"He does what is hard to do." They show up when it's inconvenient. They act with courage and care when others would turn away.

"He endures what is hard to endure." In times of tension or pain, they remain steady, patient, and kind.

"He reveals his secrets to you." There is trust, openness, and no pretense.

"He keeps your secrets." Loyalty is offered not just in words, but in silence.

"When misfortunes strike, he doesn't abandon you." Even when the world turns away, this friend stays close—rooted in compassion.

"When you're down and out, he doesn't look down on you." There is no judgment. Just presence.

In simple terms, a true friend walks beside you not only in joy, but in difficulty—giving freely, caring deeply, and holding space without turning away. This kind of friendship is rare and deeply nourishing to the heart.

Chapter 41: The Lantern Festival

Let no one bring about another's ruin
and not despise in any way or place;
Let them not wish each other any ill
from provocation or from enmity.
-The Buddha [50]

In a peaceful village by a river bend, preparations for the Lantern Festival were in progress. Villagers crafted delicate paper lanterns, each one painted with prayers for happiness and peace. But one young man named Shuta sat quietly beneath a plum tree, his lantern still blank.

An old Zen master named Yuen approached him, his steps soft on the stone path.

"Why don't you write your wish?" Yuen asked.

Soma looked down. "I don't know what to write. Everyone wishes for something—long life, success, love. I feel I should, too… but I'm not sure what's right."

Yuen smiled and took a seat beside him. "Once, I asked a child the same question. Do you know what she wrote?"

Shuta shook his head.

"She wrote, 'May no one be afraid of me.'"

Shuta's eyes widened.

Yuen continued, "To walk gently in this world—not proud, not greedy, not harsh. That's a lantern that lights more than one path."

Reflection

We often search for peace as if it were somewhere far away—a reward for success, a result of control, or the outcome of a perfect life. But peace is not a prize; it is a presence. A gentle, watchful way of moving through the world.

Like the child's quiet lantern, peace begins when we no longer wish harm—when we commit, not just to kindness in action, but to harmlessness in being. This means we walk with care, speak with softness, listen without rushing, and refrain from anything the wise would blame.

We don't need to be bold to be strong, or loud to be heard. True wholesomeness shines in simplicity: in being content, in not disturbing others, in extending love beyond familiarity—upward, downward, and across.

Pause today and ask yourself:

- Do I bring safety into a room, or tension?
- Do I allow others the space to be as they are, or do I seek to shape them to my liking?
- What would it mean to walk so gently that even my shadow doesn't stir fear?

Real-Life Application Scenario

Scenario: Parenting Through a Child's Tantrum

Your child is having a hard day—maybe tired, maybe overwhelmed. Suddenly, a small frustration explodes into a full-blown tantrum. You feel your own emotions rise. You want to stop it quickly, to make it quiet down, to correct it firmly.

But instead of reacting with impatience or control, you recall the teaching: peace begins with harmlessness. You take a breath—not to suppress your feelings, but to stay rooted in presence.

You crouch beside your child—not looming, not scolding. Your voice stays gentle. "You're upset. I see that. I'm here." No fixing, no forcing. Just a calm space where their feelings are allowed to pass like clouds across the sky.

You don't add fuel to the fire. You don't try to rush them into composure. You hold them close, not to cast light on their flaws, but to remind them they are safe.

Later, your child may not remember the details. But they will remember your warmth. Your calm. The way love didn't leave when they weren't at their best.

That is the heart of mindful presence: to love not just when others are easy, but when they are most in need of softness.

Exploring the Quote

This teaching embodies the spirit of non-harming and loving kindness.

It begins with *"Let no one bring about another's ruin."* Causing harm—whether through action, speech, or intention—goes against the heart of the Way.

"And not despise in any way or place." True compassion does not make room for contempt. No matter the situation or the person, disdain only darkens the mind.

"Let them not wish each other any ill from provocation or from enmity." Even when provoked, even in the presence of anger or old wounds, the practice is to wish no harm. In simple terms, the path of peace is not just stillness in silence but choosing again and again not to respond with hatred. Let your heart be large enough to hold even difficulty without striking back.

Chapter 42: The Two Cups

The true person is grateful and thankful, for the virtuous only know how to be grateful and thankful.

-The Buddha [1]

Under the misty pines in a serene village, lived old Ichirō, a potter with crooked hands and a kind face. People traveled from distant towns for his cups—not because they were perfect, but because they felt like they'd been made with a bow of the heart.

One morning, a young man named Daiki arrived. His tone was sharp, his robe neat, and his eyes restless.

"I hear your cups are good," he said, holding one up to the light. "But not flawless."

Ichirō smiled and said nothing.

Daiki continued, "Do you know I walked three days to get here? You should be honored."

Still, the old potter said nothing.

Daiki left with a cup but no bow, no coin, no thanks.

Later that day, a young girl returned a broken teacup Ichirō had gifted her several seasons ago. "I dropped it," she whispered, holding the pieces in her palms. "It really meant to me. Thank you."

Ichirō chuckled. "Ah, it lived a full life then." He crafted her a new one without charge. "Gratitude," he said softly, "is the glaze that makes even a cracked cup shine."

That evening, Ichirō told his apprentice:

"You'll meet two kinds of people. One believes they are owed, even when receiving. The other bows with their heart, even when empty-handed. One walks with shadows, the other with light."

He then poured tea into two cups.

Only one held the warmth.

Reflection

Gratitude is not a reaction—it's a way of seeing.

Being *ungrateful* is not merely a missed virtue; it's the mark of a life disconnected from truth. A person who takes without thanks, who expects without reverence, is like a vessel with a crack—no matter how much is poured in, it never fills.

True gratitude, like the young girl with the broken cup, doesn't wait for grand gifts. It bows to the *small*, the *simple*, the *silent*. It sees value not in perfection, but in the offering itself.

We often chase more, complain quickly, and forget the hands that quietly hold us up. But in a moment of stillness, we can remember: to receive with a whole heart is itself a sacred act.

Pause today and ask yourself:

- Am I expecting, or appreciating?
- Who have I silently depended on without ever thanking them?
- What if I let my heart bow today, even for the small things?

Real-Life Application Example

Scenario: Feeling Unseen in a Relationship

You've been showing up—doing your part in the relationship, remembering birthdays, supporting through stress, and being present. And yet… You feel unnoticed. Your efforts go unacknowledged, and the silence begins to sting. Your mind starts to narrate:

"They never appreciate me."

"Why am I always the one giving?"

You feel bitterness start to bloom. But then, a quiet memory returns—*Gratitude is the mark of the true person.*

You breathe.

Instead of closing off, you open. You gently let your partner know what you've been feeling—not in accusation, but in vulnerability.

And then, you begin a quiet shift: You thank them for the cup of tea they made, even if you asked for it. You thank them for listening, even when the conversation is messy. You thank them for just being there, sharing space with you.

Not performatively—but sincerely.

You notice that something starts changing. Their shoulders soften. They begin mirroring your words. One evening, they say, "I don't say it enough… but I'm really grateful for you."

Gratitude, once planted, grows.

Not overnight. Not loudly. But steadily.

In choosing to be the true person, even when it feels one-sided, you become the very light that helps love return home. And that is the quiet revolution of the grateful heart.

Exploring the Quote

This teaching highlights the quiet strength of gratitude.

It begins with *"The true person is grateful and thankful."* Gratitude isn't just politeness—it's the natural expression of a heart that sees clearly and humbly receives what is given.

"For the virtuous only know how to be grateful and thankful." A truly virtuous person doesn't take goodness for granted. They recognize the small kindnesses, the unseen efforts, and the gifts of life as sacred.

Gratitude softens pride and dissolves entitlement. It brings the mind back to the present, back to what is already here, already enough. It develops the faculty of compassion.

In simple terms, to be truly human is to be grateful. When the heart bows often, it walks lightly and sees the world as a blessing.

Chapter 43: The Bamboo Lesson

All are afraid of the stick, all fear death. Putting oneself in another's place, one should not beat or kill others.

-The Buddha [27]

There lived an old Zen teacher named Shoji on the edge of a bamboo forest. Each spring, he welcomed a few young students to live and train under the bamboo grove beside the temple.

One year, two students—Touba and Junpei—began quarreling over a single meditation cushion placed beneath the oldest bamboo.

"It's always been mine," Touba insisted.

"You got here after me today," Junpei countered. "I was simply quiet."

The argument grew louder, each word sharper. At last, Junpei stood and shoved Touba aside. "Then don't meditate. Go sit somewhere else!"

Touba clenched his fists and nearly struck back—but Master Shoji's voice rang through the grove.

"Come with me."

The two followed him in silence. Shoji led them to the edge of the grove where the tallest bamboo stood—scarred and cracked. He tapped it gently with his staff.

"This bamboo," he said, "grew tall because it did not strike the ones around it."

Then he handed them each a slender stick of green bamboo and said, "If you believe striking will bring you closer to awakening, then hit this tree."

They hesitated. Then tried.

The tree did not flinch. But their hands ached.

Shoji smiled. "Now switch places. Feel the stick, not as the wielder, but as the struck. And feel your fingers as an extended part of the stick."

Each took turns, striking and receiving.

When they looked at each other again, the anger had vanished.

Reflection

We often see conflict as something we must win. But every strike—physical or verbal—return to the hand that delivers it. Not immediately, perhaps, but inwardly. It bruises our clarity, hardens the heart, dulls the edge of mindfulness.

The teaching whispered through Shoji's grove is simple and profound: Feel the strike from both ends. When we lash out at another, we also injure the peace within us.

True strength is not in silencing others, but in softening ourselves.

The bamboo bends yet does not break. Similarly, the heart can also be rooted in compassion.

Pause today and ask yourself:

- Can I see myself in the one I disagree with?
- What harm comes to me when I harm another?
- How would I act if I truly felt their pain as my own?

Real-Life Application Example

Scenario: A Heated Argument with Your Partner

You're frustrated. Perhaps they forgot something important and said something sharp. Words rise to your tongue—accusation, sarcasm, the sting of "you always..." and "you never..."

But then you pause.

You recall Shoji's teaching.

"Feel your fingers as an extended part of the bamboo—when it strikes, it strikes you too."

You breathe.

Before reacting, you shift inward. You imagine their fatigue, their stress. You feel not just your own pain, but theirs.

Instead of striking, you speak gently. "I feel hurt. But I know you're hurting too."

The air softens. Walls begin to lower.

In this choice—not to lash but to listen—you protect the peace in both hearts. And in doing so, you embody the wisdom of the bamboo: strong, still, and rooted in compassion.

Exploring the Quote

This teaching invites us into the heart of compassion through direct understanding.
It begins with *"All are afraid of the stick, all fear death."* Every being values its life. Just as you recoil from pain or danger, so do all others. This is something we all share.
"Putting oneself in another's place, one should not beat or kill others." This is the root of empathy—feeling what another might feel. When you see yourself in the other, harming becomes unthinkable.
This is not merely moral advice—it is deep wisdom. When the walls between "self" and "other" soften, compassion flows naturally.
In simple terms, when you remember that others, like you, tremble before suffering and long for safety, your hands grow gentle, and your heart opens wide. This is the way of peace.

Chapter 44: The Echo

Do not speak harshly to anyone; those who are thus spoken to will retort. Malicious talk is indeed the cause of trouble (dukkha) and retribution will come to you.

-The Buddha [28]

Once, there lived a young monk named Hibiki in a mountain temple renowned for its stillness and fresh air. But Hibiki was restless. He prided himself on being clever, always ready with a biting remark or sharp correction. When others made mistakes, Hibiki would smirk and say, "I only speak the truth."

One morning, Hibiki was sent by the abbot to fetch water from the stream below. As he walked with his empty bucket, he crossed paths with Elder Akihito, who was slowly sweeping fallen petals off the stone path.

"You missed a few," Hibiki said dryly. "Aren't elders supposed to be examples?"

Akihito simply smiled and bowed slightly.

Later that afternoon, Hibiki heard giggles from two junior monks. One of them pointed at him and whispered something behind a sleeve. Hibiki's face burned. "If you have something to say, say it," he barked.

The next day, Hibiki found a note under his mat. It read: *"The bamboo grove speaks only when the wind pushes it. But your tongue moves even in stillness."*

Confused and annoyed, Hibiki stormed to the abbot. "Someone is mocking me!"

The abbot handed him a bamboo staff and pointed to the mountain trail. "Walk to the third bend where the echo is strongest. Shout what you wish to hear."

Hibiki obeyed. At the third bend, he shouted, "You are wise!"

The echo came back, "You are wise… You are wise…"

He grinned. Then, he shouted, "You're a fool!"

The echo returned, "You're a fool… you're a fool…"

Hibiki lowered his eyes.

On the way back to the monastery, he passed Akihito sweeping again. He stopped. Bowed low. "I'm sorry for my words the other day."

Akihito smiled. "Better to drop the stone in still water than throw it and wonder why there are ripples."

From that day on, Hibiki spoke more softly. And the temple grew even more silent.

Reflection

We often mistake sharp words for clarity and bold speech for truth. But Zen reminds us: it is not what we say, but how we say it—and why—that shapes the silence after.

Like the echo of what is shouted into the mountain, our words return to us in tone, in consequence, in relationship. Every harsh phrase tossed outward sends ripples across the waters of connection.

Hibiki believed honesty was enough. But honesty, without humility, becomes a sword without a sheath. Words rooted in ego bruise. Words planted in stillness nourish.

The wise speak not to correct others but to awaken them—gently, like morning light.

Pause today and ask yourself:

- Am I speaking to be right… or to be kind?
- What part of me is reaching for this word—the ego or the heart?
- Can I let silence speak for me?

Real-Life Application Example

Scenario: A Teacher's Reaction in Class

You're a teacher. A student disrupts the class for the third time that morning. Your patience wears thin, and in a moment of exasperation, you snap: "Why can't you ever just listen like everyone else?"

The room stiffens. The student lowers their eyes. You move on quickly—but something in your chest feels heavy. Later, while sitting quietly, you recall:

"Do not speak harshly to anyone… Malicious talk is indeed the cause of trouble."

You realize it wasn't the correction that caused harm—but the *tone* and *assumption*. You had scolded, not guided. You had wounded, not awakened.

That afternoon, you gently call the student aside and ask, "Is something bothering you lately? I notice you're not yourself in class."

The student hesitates… and then opens up. There's trouble at home. They haven't been sleeping. The misbehavior wasn't defiance—it was distress.

You apologize for your tone and offer support instead of scolding. The next day, the student shows up early. Quieter. More present. Something has shifted.

You learn: Discipline with compassion is a teacher's true strength. Harsh words might demand silence, but kind awareness inspires growth.

Exploring the Quote

This teaching offers a mindful reminder about the power of speech.

It begins with *"Do not speak harshly to anyone."* Words are like arrows—they can pierce deeply. Once released, they cannot be taken back.

"Those who are thus spoken to will retort." Harsh words rarely end with silence. They echo, stir anger, and invite more pain.

"Malicious talk is indeed the cause of trouble (dukkha)." When we speak to wound, we plant seeds of suffering for ourselves and others.

"And retribution will come to you." The harm we cause often comes back to haunt us. Not as punishment, but as a natural consequence.

In simple terms, speak gently. What you send out returns. A kind tongue brings peace; a harsh one, sorrow. Choose the way that quiets the heart.

Practice Meditation: The Soft Cup of Loving-Kindness

1. **Settle the Body.**

Sit quietly. Let your hands rest open in your lap. Feel the breath rise and fall, like gentle waves. You are here. There is nothing to fix. Nothing to prove.

2. **Begin with Gratitude.**

Say "gently" to yourself with mindfulness and inward focus:

Thank you, breath, for returning.

Thank you, Dhamma, for being present.

Thank you, heart, for listening—however quietly.

I thank myself for arriving.

I thank myself for practicing.

3. **Forgive Gently.**

Let the heart soften and say "gently" to yourself with mindfulness and inward focus:

I forgive myself for the moments I was careless.

I forgive myself for not knowing better.

I am learning. I will keep learning.

I forgive those who harmed me, knowingly or unknowingly.

I forgive the careless, the angry, the lost.

I see their pain. I let go of the weight.

4. **Offer Loving-Kindness.**

Now begin to offer gentle wishes with mindfulness and inward focus:

a) To yourself first:

May I be happy.

May I be peaceful.

May I be free from all suffering.

b) To someone you love (name them if you like):

May you be happy.

May you be peaceful.

May you be free from all suffering.

c) To everyone in your home:

Repeat for each person, one at a time—no rush. Hold them gently in your heart and offer:

May you be happy. May you be free.

d) Extend Outward: To all the plants, minerals, and silent lives in your home:

May you be nourished.

May you be peaceful.

May you be liberated.

e) To unseen beings—near or far:

May you be happy.

May you be free.

f) To all creatures on earth, in the air, and in the sea:

May you be safe.

May you be peaceful.

May you be liberated.

g) To all beings in all realms of existence:

May you be happy.

May you be peaceful.

May you be liberated, liberated, liberated.

5. Return and Rest.

Feel the quiet warmth in your heart. Let it expand like sunlight through morning mist.

Breathe in, breathe out. Stay soft.

Say silently:

May Dhamma grow. May all be well.

You are the cup. You are the pouring. Let yourself be empty and full at once.

Part 8: Trusting Your Own Way Forward

Hello, Seeker of Still Light,

Sometimes, we wait for the path to be revealed in full, like a scroll unrolling with all the answers. But the way forward is rarely so loud. It arrives in glimpses, like the glow of a bamboo lantern on a moonless night.

In this part of the journey, we are invited not to chase clarity, but to *become it*. To walk not because we know the destination, but because our step is honest. To trust not because the road is smooth, but because our heart is steady.

You've walked through silence, acceptance, and compassion. Now you arrive at a gentle truth:

You do not need more proof. You only need to keep walking.

These stories offer something valuable: confidence in your inner lantern and trust in the way your feet meet the earth.

Here's what you'll explore:

- **The Courage of Inner Trust**: How to move through uncertainty with quiet power
- **Stories of Invisible Strength**: Moments where discernment, patience, and faith become our true compass
- **Practices for Walking Forward, Gently**: Tools to help you live from what's steady and true—right where you are

You don't need a blazing trail. A single quiet flame is enough.

The teachings now live inside you. The wisdom has walked beside you. And every step from here forward is your own.

Let's begin—again.

Chapter 45: The Bamboo Lantern

Like the Himalayas, the good are visible even from afar; like arrows shot in the night, the wicked are not seen even though they may be near.

-The Buddha [37]

In a seaside town, a young woman named Emi lived. She had married into a wealthy family known for their lavish offerings to wandering teachers. Yet no matter how many philosophers came and went, Emi always felt something was missing—a quiet clarity she had glimpsed as a child when she once sat in the presence of a renowned Zen master. Her husband and in-laws often urged her to host the respected teachers they favored. She obeyed respectfully, but her heart never stirred.

One moonless night, while tending the courtyard lanterns, Emi felt a deep longing. She placed a single bamboo lantern on a smooth stone and whispered into the darkness:

"This light carries the gratitude I've held in my heart for so long. Its glow is my wish to meet again the teacher whose words first showed me the way."

She lit the lantern, and as the flame caught, a breeze lifted it gently skyward. It rose higher and higher until it disappeared among the stars.

In the morning, Emi's family was astonished when word spread through the town: the renowned Zen master Dai himself was approaching with his disciples, traveling across land and water, drawn by a heartfelt call.

When he arrived, the Zen master spoke quietly to the gathered villagers:

"When the mind is clear and the heart is sincere, even the smallest gesture can cross any distance."

Emi's in-laws, moved by the grace of his presence, bowed in respect. And for the first time, they understood the quiet power that had always lived in her devotion.

Later, as she tended the embers of the lantern, Emi smiled. She had always believed that no matter where you are, true faith is never far away.

Reflection

Sometimes, we believe our sincerity must be loud to be heard, our devotion must be grand to be real. But Emi's story reminds us that even the quietest gesture—a single lantern, a single thought—can bridge distances we can't measure.

When the heart is clear, its light travels further than we realize. True connection doesn't rely on spectacle or force. It grows from the simple courage to honor what matters most to you, even if no one else sees it right away.

In this way, faith becomes a lantern of its own: steady, warm, and quietly luminous.

Pause today and ask yourself:

- What simple gesture could I offer to honor what I value most?
- Where have I been waiting for recognition instead of trusting my own sincerity?
- What would it feel like to believe my devotion is already enough?

Real-Life Application Example

Scenario: Feeling Unseen at Work or in a Group

Imagine you are part of a project or a community where your ideas are often overlooked. You keep showing up with care, but it feels like no one notices.

Instead of forcing others to validate your efforts, you pause and remember Emi's lantern. You write a thoughtful note to a colleague, share resources that helped you, or quietly support the work without expecting applause.

Days or weeks later, you discover your consistency has inspired someone you didn't even realize was watching.

In that moment, you see how the simplest gestures, offered sincerely and without expectation, have their own power to connect and uplift. Your steady light was never wasted. It simply took time to be seen.

Exploring the Quote

This quote describes how goodness naturally reveals itself.

It begins with *"Like the Himalayas, the good are visible even from afar."* A person of integrity stands out clearly, just as great mountains rise above the land. Their virtue shines no matter where you are.

"Like arrows shot in the night, the wicked are not seen even though they may be near." Those who act with deceit or harm often remain hidden, like arrows in the darkness. You may overlook their influence right away.

In simple terms, genuine goodness is unmistakable, while hidden harm often remains unseen until it strikes.

Chapter 46: The Lantern of Seeing

Four noble truths? There is the case where he discerns, as it has come to be, that 'This is stress... This is the origination of stress... This is the cessation of stress... This is the way leading to the cessation of stress.

-The Buddha [39]

In a quiet mountain temple, a young student named Kaoru approached the Zen master after evening meditation.

“Master,” Kaoru began, voice unsteady, “why does life feel so heavy, even when everything seems fine?”

The master motioned for Kaoru to follow. They stepped into the garden, where an old lantern rested beside the path.

“Pick up this lantern,” the master instructed.

Kaoru lifted it easily.

“Now walk with it.”

Kaoru circled the garden, puzzled.

“Tell me,” the master said, “is the lantern heavy?”

“No,” Kaoru replied, “it's very light.”

The master nodded. “And if you carried it all day and all night?”

Kaoru frowned. “Then it would feel heavy indeed.”

“This,” said the master, “is how suffering works. Even small burdens—expectations, attachments, cravings—grow heavy when we never put them down.”

Kaoru lowered the lantern to the ground and exhaled.

“But how do I set it down?” Kaoru asked softly.

The master crouched beside the lantern. “First, see clearly what you are carrying. Aging... illness... death... sorrow, lamentation, pain, distress, and despair. This is suffering.”

He held up four fingers.

"First," he said, "acknowledge that there is suffering in life. Birth, aging, illness, death, sorrow, lamentation, pain, distress, and despair—this is the nature of the world."

One finger folded down.

"Then, see what gives rise to it—this grasping for what pleases you, this fear of what you cannot control."

Second finger folded down.

"Next, see that there is an end to it, like setting down this lantern. Freedom is possible."

The third finger folded.

"And finally," the master said, "walk the path that leads you there: right understanding, intention, speech, action, livelihood, effort, mindfulness, and concentration. Which means… There is a way to end the suffering."

The last fingers folded gently into his palm.

Kaoru looked at the lantern on the path, no longer burdened by his hands. In that small, moonlit moment, he understood:

To see the weight clearly is the beginning of release. To walk the path is to remember that suffering is neither punishment nor destiny—it is simply something that can be laid aside.

And with that knowing, Kaoru bowed deeply.

Reflection

Sometimes, we think suffering means something has gone terribly wrong. But in truth, it simply means we are alive and feeling the weight of being human.

The Four Noble Truths remind us that the heaviness we carry isn't personal failure—it is the natural tension of craving, clinging, and resisting what is.

When we pause to see this clearly, a quiet courage appears. We realize we don't have to keep grasping for what we wish would happen or fighting against what already has.

Freedom begins the moment we stop blaming ourselves for the lantern in our hands and instead ask: *Can I gently put this down?*

Pause today and ask yourself:

- What am I carrying that has quietly grown too heavy?
- Which craving or fear is fueling this burden?

- What small step could I take to set it down and walk a little lighter?

Real-Life Application Example

Scenario: Facing Rejection at an Interview

Imagine you have poured your energy into applying for a role you truly wanted. You felt certain this opportunity would finally bring validation and security. But the call comes: *"We've chosen another candidate."*

First, you notice the tightness in your chest—the sorrow, the frustration, the sense of being unseen. Instead of turning away, you acknowledge: *This is suffering.*

You breathe, feeling the craving beneath the pain—wanting recognition, fearing worthlessness. You see clearly that this grasping fuels the ache.

Then, you remember: this disappointment is not the whole of who you are. It is a passing experience, not a life sentence. You decide to let go of the story that you must achieve something to be enough. You remind yourself that your path is not defined by a single outcome.

And as you do, a soft spaciousness opens. You feel lighter, more able to take the next step, without the weight of needing life to be exactly as you planned.

Exploring the Quote

This quote describes the Four Noble Truths, the heart of the path to freedom.

The Four Noble Truths are a framework for understanding suffering and the path to liberation:

1. "This is stress." (Dukkha) — Recognizing Suffering

- All beings experience suffering.
- This suffering includes:
    - Physical pain
    - Emotional disappointment
    - Dissatisfaction and frustration
- The first step is to see and accept this truth rather than deny or avoid it.

2. "This is the origination of stress." (Samudaya) — Understanding the Cause

- Suffering arises because of specific causes:
    - Craving (tanha) – the constant wanting and grasping for pleasure or avoidance of discomfort
    - Clinging – attachment to ideas, people, possessions, or identities
    - Ignorance – not seeing reality as it is
- When we see how these forces operate, we understand why suffering keeps recurring.

3. "This is the cessation of stress." (Nirodha) — Realizing the End of Suffering

- If craving and clinging end, suffering also ends.
- This is not merely a temporary pause but:
    - The total dissolving of all grasping and confusion
    - A state of inner peace that is steady and unshaken by success or loss

4. "This is the way leading to the cessation of stress." (Magga) — The Path

- The Buddha taught a practical path to freedom called the Noble Eightfold Path:
    - *Right View* – seeing reality and the Four Noble Truths clearly
    - *Right Intention* – cultivating intentions of renunciation, goodwill, and harmlessness
    - *Right Speech* – speaking truthfully and kindly
    - *Right Action* – acting ethically and compassionately
    - *Right Livelihood* – earning a living in a way that does not harm
    - *Right Effort* – making consistent effort to develop wholesome qualities
    - *Right Mindfulness* – maintaining awareness of body, feelings, mind, and phenomena
    - *Right Concentration* – developing deep states of meditative focus

In simple terms

- This teaching shows that suffering is neither inevitable nor permanent.
- By understanding its cause and following the path, one can experience liberation and lasting peace.

Chapter 47: The Bamboo Path

The Noble Eightfold Path? Right view, right resolve, right speech, right action, right livelihood, right effort, right mindfulness, right concentration.

-The Buddha [49]

Once, in a small mountain village, there lived an elderly potter named Daisetsu. Though his hands were wrinkled and his back bent, he was known for crafting bowls so fine they seemed to hold not only tea but quietness itself.

One evening, a young woman named Kana came to his workshop. Her eyes were tired; her mind tangled in sorrow. She bowed deeply.

"Master," she said, "I have read many sutras, chanted many verses, but still my heart is restless. Please—tell me what path I must follow to find peace."

Daisetsu smiled gently. Without a word, he took up a bamboo pole and set it across two stones in the garden.

"Kana," he asked, "can you walk across this?"

She looked uncertain. "It is very narrow."

"Indeed," he said. "But it is strong."

He tapped the bamboo with his staff. "This bamboo is the Eightfold Path. Not too wide to invite distraction, not too thin to break under you. Every step must be placed with care."

He raised one finger.

"The first step is right view—seeing clearly that there is sorrow, and that clinging gives it power."

A second finger.

"Then right resolve—choosing renunciation, kindness, and harmlessness over habit."

A third finger.

"Right speech—words that heal, not wound."

A fourth.

"Right action—living in a way that harms no creature."

A fifth.

"Right livelihood—work that nourishes without deceit."

A sixth.

"Right effort—tending your mind as you would a garden, pulling out the weeds again and again."

A seventh.

"Right mindfulness—remaining present, whether joy or sorrow arises."

And finally, his eighth finger lifted.

"Right concentration—stilling the heart so it becomes clear water."

He set down his hand. The bamboo pole gleamed in the moonlight.

"When you walk this path," Daisetsu said softly, "step by step, moment by moment, you will discover the peace that has always waited within you."

Kana felt her breathing slow. The night air seemed lighter. She bowed again, and for the first time in many months, her mind was quiet.

Reflection

Sometimes we think wisdom must be complicated, hidden in many teachings. But the Eightfold Path is really just a set of clear, steady steps.

Each part—right understanding, intention, speech, action, livelihood, effort, mindfulness, and concentration—helps you live in a way that is kind, honest, and peaceful.

You don't have to master them all at once. You only need to keep walking, step by step, coming back whenever you wander.

It is like walking along a garden path. Some parts are smooth. Others are rocky. But every part is part of the same way forward.

Pause today and ask yourself:

- Which of these eight steps feels easiest for me to practice?
- Which one feels hardest?
- What is one simple way I could bring more balance or care into my day?

Real-Life Application Example

Scenario: Deciding Whether to Change Your Job

Imagine you are thinking about leaving your job. You feel stuck and unhappy, but you are also afraid to make a change.

Instead of trying to figure everything out at once, you could gently follow the Eightfold Path:

- *Right view:* Be honest about how you feel. Notice your stress without hiding from it.
- *Right intention:* Set your purpose. "I want to find work that is good for me and others."
- *Right speech:* Talk about your plans in a truthful, respectful way. Do not gossip or curse your present moment.
- *Right action:* Take small, steady steps—like updating your resume or talking to trusted mentors.
- *Right livelihood:* Consider jobs that match your values.
- *Right effort:* Keep going even when you feel uncertain.
- *Right mindfulness:* Pay attention to your thoughts and emotions without judging them.
- *Right concentration:* Take quiet time each day to calm your mind.

When you approach your choice this way, you don't feel so rushed or overwhelmed. You see that every step can be taken with care, and that walking slowly is still walking forward.

Exploring the Quote

This quote describes the Noble Eightfold Path, the way to freedom and peace.

The Eight Parts of the Path:

1. Right View

- Seeing things as they are, before ideas about them arise.
- Recognizing impermanence, suffering, and no fixed self.

- Understanding the Four Noble Truths about suffering, its cause, its end, and the way to end it.

2. Right Resolve

- Setting your heart on good intentions.
- Committing to goodwill, harmlessness, and letting go of grasping and ill will.

3. Right Speech

- Speaking truthfully.
- Using kind, respectful words that create understanding and harmony.

4. Right Action

- Acting ethically.
- Acting from clarity rather than habit.
- Doing what brings no regret, causing no harm to yourself and others.

5. Right Livelihood

- Earning your living in ways that do not cause suffering or exploitation.
- Choosing work that is honest and compassionate.

6. Right Effort

- Preventing and letting go of unwholesome habits.
- Gently but firmly turning the mind toward what is wholesome.
- Not straining or forcing, just returning again and again.

7. Right Mindfulness

- Abiding in awareness of body, feeling, mind, and phenomena.
- Not clinging to thoughts or pushing them away—just seeing.
- Observing with clarity instead of reacting automatically.

8. Right Concentration

- Developing steady, focused attention through meditation.
- Cultivating deep states of calm and insight.
- Allowing the mind to become stable and quiet.
- Resting in the stillness beneath all movement.

In simple terms

- These eight qualities work together like stepping stones.
- They guide you gently from confusion to clarity, and from stress to deep peace.

Chapter 48: The Lantern in the Cellar

Clear knowing is the leader in the attainment of skillful qualities,
followed by conscience & concern.
-The Buddha [48]

There was a young man named Itsuki in a small city who inherited a vast house from his grandfather. The house was sturdy and beautiful, but it had a dark cellar no one liked to enter.

Itsuki began to store things there—old tools, jars, scraps of broken furniture—until the cellar became so crowded he could barely step inside. One day, he went down to retrieve a pot, stumbled in the darkness, and cut his hand on a shard of glass.

Fuming, he climbed back upstairs and complained to the village's Zen master, who was sipping tea under a cypress tree.

"The cellar is cursed," Itsuki grumbled. "No matter how careful I am, I hurt myself every time."

The master looked at him kindly.

"Have you ever tried to bring a lantern?"

Itsuki blinked.

"I thought it wouldn't matter. It's only a cellar."

The master smiled.

"It is precisely because it is dark that you must bring a light."

He touched Itsuki's bandaged hand.

"Ignorance is like that darkness—whatever you do inside it grows tangled and painful."

That evening, Itsuki carried a lantern down the steps. For the first time, he saw the cellar clearly: the shelves, the jars, the hidden corners where the broken things lay. He began to tidy them with quiet confidence.

He thought of the master's words and laughed softly to himself: "Nothing is cursed—only unseen."

Reflection

Sometimes we keep stumbling over the same troubles in our lives—old patterns, reactions, regrets—and we tell ourselves, *"This is just how things are."*

Itsuki's story shows us that ignorance is like a dark cellar. When we act without a clear understanding, confusion and suffering multiply. We become tangled in fear, blame, or habit. But when we bring the lantern of awareness—when we look honestly and patiently—things that once seemed cursed reveal themselves as simply *unseen*.

Awareness is not always comfortable at first. But it is the beginning of freedom. Clear knowing leads to wise choices. Wise choices pave the way for a life of peace and confidence.

Pause today and ask yourself:

- What part of your life feels dark or confusing right now?
- What might you see if you gently shined the light of awareness there?
- How would your actions change if you understood more fully what you were meeting?

Real-Life Application Scenario

Scenario: Clarifying a Difficult Relationship

Perhaps you have a relationship that feels painful or stuck—maybe with a colleague, a parent, or a partner. You keep reacting in the same ways, saying the same words, feeling the same disappointments.

It can seem like that cellar—crowded, dark, unmanageable.

Instead of trying to force a solution or blame yourself or the other person, bring a lantern of clear seeing: Set aside time to reflect calmly on what is actually happening. Notice the patterns: What do you feel? What do you fear? What do you long for? Ask yourself which of your actions come from old habits, and which arise from understanding.

As you look honestly, you may see what has been hidden—old wounds, unspoken needs, misunderstandings. From there, your next steps become clearer.

Awareness doesn't magically fix everything overnight, but it transforms the energy of confusion into the possibility of wise, compassionate action.

Sometimes, all that is needed is the courage to carry a light into the places you have not yet dared to see.

Exploring the Quote

This teaching describes how wholesome qualities take root and grow.

It begins with *"Clear knowing is the leader in the attainment of skillful qualities."* Awareness and understanding come first. When you see clearly, you can choose wisely.

"Followed by conscience and concern." Conscience is the quiet voice that feels when something is unwholesome. Concern is caring about the well-being of yourself and others.

In simple terms, a clear understanding lights the path, and a caring heart keeps you steady as you walk.

Chapter 49: The Bridge in the Rain

There are these five powers. What five? Faith, conscience, prudence, energy, and wisdom.

-The Buddha [13]

In a mountain village where the clouds loved to rest, a wooden bridge crossed a wide, cold river. The villagers used it every day, but during the rainy season, the river would swell, and many feared the crossing.

One morning, a traveler named Taiki arrived. He watched as the villagers gathered on one side of the river, hesitant to cross. The bridge creaked and swayed. The clouds hung low. Taiki stepped forward.

"Why do you wait?" he asked.

An old man replied, "The river is angry today. The bridge might not hold."

Taiki bowed gently. "Then let me try. If I fall, you'll know to stay. If I make it, you'll know it can be done."

Before he stepped onto the bridge, he closed his eyes. He found a quiet steadiness in his chest, like trusting the path, even without knowing where it would lead.

A sense of rightness followed, reminding him this wasn't about proving anything, but walking with care.

He placed each step with attention and patience.

When the wind pushed back, something deeper kept him moving forward.

And when he neared the middle, a soft understanding arose: every crossing in life feels like this. You don't wait for stillness—you learn to move with grace through the storm.

He reached the other side. One by one, the villagers followed.

From that day on, they referred to it as "The Bridge of Five Steps."

Reflection

In uncertain times, we often wait for perfect conditions. We pause at the edge, hoping the wind will settle or the river will shrink. But life rarely offers perfect crossings.

Instead, we are invited to walk forward with our quiet inner strengths—the five powers that guide the heart.

- **Faith** helps us begin.
- **Conscience** keeps us honest.
- **Prudence** teaches patience.
- **Energy** gives us momentum.
- **Wisdom** reveals what truly matters.

Together, they help us move through the storms—not untouched, but unshaken.

Pause today and ask:

- Where in my life am I standing at a crossroads?
- Which of these five powers do I need to strengthen at this time?
- What might shift if I took one step, not with certainty, but with trust?

Real-Life Application Example

Scenario: Starting a New Chapter in Job

You've been offered an opportunity, but with it comes risk. New responsibilities. The fear of failure. The temptation to wait "until the time feels right."

Instead, try stepping onto the "bridge" with the five powers:

1. **Faith** – Trust your intention. You don't need to know every answer. Begin with a sincere heart.
2. **Conscience** – Ask yourself, "Is this in alignment with what I value?" Let that be your compass.
3. **Prudence** – Make a thoughtful plan. Speak to mentors. Learn what you can without overthinking.
4. **Energy** – Take the first step. Then the second. Let movement carry you through fear.
5. **Wisdom** – Let go of control. Let your experience, not your fear, be your teacher.

Even when life feels like a stormy crossing, these inner powers are your steady handrails. Use them wisely, and you'll find not only where the bridge takes you but also who you become along the way.

Exploring the Quote

This teaching points to five quiet strengths that support the path of awakening.

It begins with *"Faith."* Not blind belief, but a deep trust in the possibility of inner freedom and the path that leads there.

"Conscience." The gentle voice within that knows when we're straying, that urges us to live with honesty and care.

"Prudence." Also called moral concern or wise fear. It's the awareness of cause and effect—the care to avoid what leads to harm.

"Energy." The steady courage to keep going, to choose what is skillful even when it's not easy.

"Wisdom." Clear seeing. Knowing what leads to peace and what does not.

In simple terms, these five powers are not loud. They don't need to be. Together, they hold the heart steady and guide it home.

Chapter 50: The Quiet Treasures

These seven treasures are not open to fire, flood, kings, thieves, or hateful heirs. Which seven? The treasure of conviction, the treasure of virtue, the treasure of conscience, the treasure of concern, the treasure of listening, the treasure of generosity, the treasure of discernment.

-The Buddha [14]

In a quiet valley beneath snow-touched ridges, young Kenshin sat beside Aya, the old caretaker of the temple gardens. Spring had come, but his heart was restless.

"Aya," he asked, stirring his tea, "is it true that Lord Migara owns a mountain of gold?"

She nodded. "So, they say. Chests full of silver too."

Kenshin sighed. "Imagine having all that. I wouldn't worry anymore."

Aya looked up from pruning the bonsai. "And if fire came? Or flood? Or someone stronger took it away?"

Kenshin frowned. "Then I'd have nothing."

Aya poured more tea and said gently, "Some treasures don't shine. But they steady the heart, wake you kindly in the morning, and ask nothing in return."

Kenshin leaned in, curious.

She didn't list them all at once; instead, she allowed them to emerge gradually, like quiet tea leaves in a kettle:

A trust that doesn't shake in hard times.

A way of living that harms no one.

A whisper of conscience that stirs before dawn.

A heart that gives without needing thanks.

Ears that listen more than they speak.

A hand that opens.

And eyes that see things just as they are.

Kenshin was silent.

Aya smiled. "If you carry these, you won't fear fire or thieves. No one can steal what's rooted deep within."
Kenshin bowed. "Then I'll begin with one."
Aya nodded. "One is enough, if you walk it fully."

Reflection

We often look for treasure outside ourselves—in what we own, how we are seen, or what we can store up for later. But in stillness, we may begin to notice that the most enduring treasures are not held in vaults or hands, but in the heart.
Trust that remains steady even when life sways. A virtue that doesn't require praise. Conscience that softly awakens us, encouraging careful living. Compassion that gives more than it takes. Listening that patiently holds space without haste to fix. Generosity that leaves no debt unpaid. Wisdom that perceives clearly, even in confusion.
These inner treasures do not rust. No fire can burn them. No thief can steal them. And no world change can diminish their worth. Even one tended well is wealth beyond measure.
Pause today and ask yourself:

- What treasure have I been chasing that doesn't last?
- Which of these quiet treasures already lives in me?
- How can I nurture just one of them today, like a small flame in the wind?

Real-Life Application Example

Scenario: Feeling Insecure in a Competitive World
Imagine you're surrounded by peers who seem to have more—more money, more status, more praise. Maybe you're tempted to measure your worth by what you lack.
But then you remember Aya's words: some treasures do not shine, but they do not disappear.
So instead of pushing harder, you begin each morning with one intention—perhaps to practice deeper listening, or to respond to stress with patience instead of haste. You may

offer kindness without waiting to be noticed, or choose to speak truthfully, even if it costs you approval.

Each act becomes a step toward quiet wealth.

By walking this path, you begin to sense a calm richness inside. You no longer feel the need to grasp or prove. What you carry is enough. You live not to outshine, but to be steady, warm, and awake.

And slowly, others may notice—not your gold, but your presence.

Exploring the Quote

This teaching describes seven inner treasures that cannot be taken, burned, or lost.

It begins with *"These seven treasures are not open to fire, flood, kings, thieves, or hateful heirs."* Unlike gold or land, these treasures are beyond the reach of the world's destruction. No one can steal what lives quietly within the heart.

"The treasure of conviction." Deep trust in the path and the truth it reveals.

"The treasure of virtue." A life rooted in honesty, harmlessness, and ethical conduct.

"The treasure of conscience." That subtle awareness within instinctively avoids harm.

"The treasure of concern." The wish to live in a way that does not burden oneself or others.

"The treasure of listening." Openness to learn, to receive, and to truly hear.

"The treasure of generosity." A giving heart, free from grasping.

"The treasure of discernment." Clear seeing—knowing what matters and what leads to peace.

In simple terms, these treasures don't shine in the sun, but they light the way from within. When protected and nurtured, they offer a wealth no one can take away.

Practice Meditation: The Path That Walks Itself

1. **Begin in Stillness**

Sit comfortably in a posture that is relaxed, upright, and grounded. Let your hands rest softly, your gaze lowered, or your eyes gently closed. Let this moment be your teacher. Take a few natural breaths. No need to control. Just return to what is already here.

2. **Settle Into the Breath**

Begin gently counting the breath: Inhale. Exhale.

When thoughts arise (and they will), notice them, bow to them, and return to the breath—again and again. This is walking the path. Let the breath be the trail you trust. You don't need to know the destination.

3. **Notice What Arises**

As the breath settles, let the heart remain open. Observe thoughts, sensations, and emotions as they arise. Don't chase. Don't judge. See each as a guest—temporary, passing, known by awareness.

If something returns again and again—pause, give it space, and just sit with it. Let it be seen. Let it soften.

4. **Feel the Ground Beneath You**

Trust the ground you are sitting on. It does not ask questions. It only supports. In the same way, trust the silence. You don't need to understand everything. You only need to stay present for the unfolding.

Let each breath, each pause, each return… be your act of faith.

5. **Trust the Path Within You**

Know silently:

I am not behind. I am not lost. The way is not elsewhere. It is here.

There is no map more accurate than your own breath. No compass more faithful than your own clarity. No teacher closer than the stillness within you.

6. **End With Loving-Kindness**

To complete your sitting, let the heart expand softly.

Silently say:

May I be happy.

May I be peaceful.

May I walk my path with trust.

Now offer outward:

May all beings—seen and unseen, far and near—be happy.

May all beings be safe, peaceful, and free.

May all beings walk their path in kindness.

Let this final breath be a gentle bow: To the path. To all beings. To yourself.

Remember:

You are the forest. You are the traveler. You are the trail.

When you sit in stillness, the whole world walks with you.

Conclusion: Whispers That Stay

"Living the Zen Way Every Day"

"When you realize nothing is lacking, the whole world belongs to you."—Lao Tzu

---

Hello, Kind Companion,

The forest never shouted. It never demanded. It simply *was*—steady in its silence, alive in its stillness.

And in that stillness, something within you began to soften, settle, and see.

Not because the world became quieter, but because *you did.*

You've discovered that peace isn't some distant peak to conquer—it's the hush between thoughts, the kindness in small gestures, the light in a bamboo lantern lifted with care.

Zen didn't hand you answers. It handed you presence.

And in that presence, you met your own truth—not as something to figure out, but something to return to.

What You've Planted

Through these fifty quiet lanterns, you've:

- Learned how a simple pause can restore clarity
- Sat with emotions without rushing them away
- Bowed to impermanence instead of bracing against it
- Walked the Eightfold Path not as a task list, but as a rhythm
- Listened beyond words—into the pulse of silence
- Given compassion its rightful boundary: wisdom
- Laid down what was too heavy and stepped forward, lighter
- Recognized that your greatest treasures cannot be stolen

These aren't lessons to memorize. They are seeds now resting in your soil. They know when and how to bloom.

Now, What Next?

Zen doesn't ask you to retreat from life. It only asks you to *show up*—fully, humbly, and awake. That doesn't mean you won't stumble. It means you'll meet your stumble with kindness.

From here forward, perhaps you'll find Zen in…

- The breath you feel before answering a difficult question
- The walk you take with no destination, only presence
- The sip of tea that warms not just your hands, but your mind
- The silent bow you offer the moment, just as it is

You don't need to become anyone else. You've only ever needed to become *aware.*

And you are.

Thank you for walking this path. For listening, not just to the stories—but to the stillness they led you back to.

If ever you feel lost again, come back to the forest.

Not to be guided—but to remember.

May your path be gentle.

May your lantern never dim.

May you be happy.

May you be peaceful.

May you trust your quiet treasures.

With gratitude always,

Your Fellow Traveler

Sati…

Final Practice Meditation: The 5-Minute Zen Return

Each time life feels loud again, you can return here—a simple practice to reconnect with presence, soften the mind, and remember you are already enough.
(This meditation is also included in your audio list so you can listen anytime.)

***

Find a quiet place. Sit comfortably—cross-legged on a cushion or upright on a chair.
Let your spine be naturally erect—not stiff, not slack—just alive and awake.
Let your hands rest gently on your lap or knees. Close your eyes lightly.
Breathe in… and out…
Let the body settle. Let the mind arrive.

Bring awareness to this moment.
You don't need to become anything. You are already here.
Just be with what is.

Now bring your attention to the breath.
Just your natural breath—no need to control it.
Notice where you feel it most clearly.
It might be the tip of your nose, the rising and falling of the chest, or the belly.
Let the breath be your anchor.

Inhale…
Exhale…
One breath at a time.

Thoughts may come. That's okay.
Notice them. Let them pass like clouds in the sky.
Gently bring your awareness back… to the breath.

Again, and again… returning to this breath.
Not the last one. Not the next one.
Just… this… one.

Now, observe the breath with greater clarity.
Notice its texture. Its rhythm.
Coolness on the in-breath. Warmth on the out-breath.
Feel the breath living you.
You don't have to do anything. Just allow.

Silence is not the absence of sound.
Silence is the absence of resistance.

Be like a mountain: steady, unmoved.
Let the breath flow like a breeze across its surface.

If thoughts come, simply smile at them.
Then come back… to the breath.

Now, begin to soften your focus.
Let the breath remain in the background.
Let awareness expand to include the whole body.
Feel the body breathing.
Feel the presence of sitting.
No effort. Just being.

You are not separate from the breath.
Not separate from this moment.
Not separate from life.

You are simply… awareness.
Open. Receptive. At ease.

Let everything be as it is.
The sounds. The sensations. The silence.

This is the heart of Zen:
Nothing to do. Nowhere to go.
Just this. Just now.

Begin to return your attention to the room around you.
Feel the ground beneath you.
Notice the temperature on your skin.
Become aware of your hands, your feet, your breath.

Take a moment to offer a quiet bow of gratitude—
To yourself. To the breath. To this moment of stillness.

When you're ready… gently open your eyes.

Carry this awareness with you—not just in stillness,
But in every step, every breath, every moment of life.

***

Continuing the Journey

Hello, Peace Seeker,

Yīng Huā Forest was never just a place. It was a whisper. A quiet vision to welcome those who seek stillness, not in escape, but in presence.

Whispers of the Zen Forest is one small path in that larger forest—a sanctuary where books breathe, tea warms, and silence teaches. Where seekers gather not to become more, but to return home to what has always been.

There is no dogma here. No rigid form. This forest welcomes you—not as a visitor, but as one who belongs. And the path continues—softly, simply, step by step.

Your Gentle Gifts

To support your unfolding, you are invited to receive:

- **You Got This** – Mindful Reflections Journal: Gentle prompts to explore your thoughts after each story
- **Mandala Coloring Book:** Creative, soothing designs to relax your mind
- **Audio Tracks:** Calming music and guided narrations for rest and reflection

You're warmly welcome to join our shared space from time to time— **freely offered** for those walking the path with sincerity:

- **30 minutes of meditation** (guided or silent)
- **30 minutes of Dhamma reflection** to deepen understanding.

These invitations are shared through the **Yīng Huā Forest Newsletter**—a quiet leaf in your inbox, carrying reflections, updates, and gentle inspiration.

Scan the QR code to receive your gifts and stay connected.

SCAN ME

May your days be spacious.

May your steps be soft.

May your forest always be nearby.

With gratitude and peace,

Sati

A Gentle Bow of Thanks

Hello, Mindful Reader

Thank you for walking with this book—for pausing, breathing, and listening between its pages.

If even one story offered you stillness, or one reflection stirred something true within you, I'm quietly grateful.

If your heart feels moved, I invite you to share a few words in a review. Your review—however simple—helps others find their way here, just as you did. It is like placing a small lantern along the path for someone still searching.

Scan the QR code below to leave a review.

SCAN ME

>> Leave a Review on Amazon<<

Thank you for being part of this quiet journey.

May your days unfold with clarity, warmth, and deep peace.

Bibliography

1. *AN 2.32–41: Samacittavagga: The Chapter on the Peaceful Mind (Translated from Pali by Bhikkhu Sujato)*. (n.d.). SuttaCentral. Retrieved July 18, 2025, from https://suttacentral.net/an2.32-41/en/sujato
2. *AN 3.15: Rathakara (Pacetana) Sutta: The Chariot Maker (Translated from the Pali by Thanissaro Bhikkhu)*. (n.d.). Accesstoinsight.org. Retrieved July 2, 2025, from https://www.accesstoinsight.org/tipitaka/an/an03/an03.015.than.html
3. *AN 3.34: Hatthaka Sutta: To Hatthaka (excerpt) On Sleeping Well in the Cold Forest (Translated from the Pali by Thanissaro Bhikkhu)*. (n.d.). Dhammatalks.org. Retrieved July 2, 2025, from https://www.dhammatalks.org/suttas/AN/AN3_35.html
4. *AN 3.65: Kalama sutta: To the kalamas (Translated from Pali by Thanissaro Bhikkhu)*. (n.d.). Accesstoinsight.org. Retrieved July 13, 2025, from https://www.accesstoinsight.org/tipitaka/an/an03/an03.065.than.html
5. *AN 3.67: Kathavatthu sutta: Topics for discussion (Translated from Pali by Thanissaro Bhikkhu)*. (n.d.). Accesstoinsight.org. Retrieved July 13, 2025, from https://www.accesstoinsight.org/tipitaka/an/an03/an03.067.than.html
6. *AN 3.69: Mula sutta: Roots (Translated from Pali by Thanissaro Bhikkhu)*. (n.d.). Accesstoinsight.org. Retrieved July 13, 2025, from https://www.accesstoinsight.org/tipitaka/an/an03/an03.069.than.html
7. *AN 3.100: Loṇakapallasutta: 10. A Lump of Salt (Translated from the Pali by Thanissaro Bhikkhu);* (n.d.). SuttaCentral. Retrieved July 2, 2025, from https://suttacentral.net/an3.100/en/sujato?lang=en&layout=plain&reference=none&notes=asterisk&highlight=false&script=latin
8. *AN 4.42: Pañha sutta: Questions (Translated from Pali by Thanissaro Bhikkhu)*. (n.d.). Accesstoinsight.org. Retrieved July 15, 2025, from https://www.accesstoinsight.org/tipitaka/an/an04/an04.042.than.html
9. *AN 5.57: Upajjhatthana sutta: Subjects for contemplation (Translated from Pali by Thanissaro Bhikkhu)*. (n.d.). Accesstoinsight.org. Retrieved July 16, 2025, from https://www.accesstoinsight.org/tipitaka/an/an05/an05.057.than.html
10. *AN 5.141: Avajānātisutta: At Tikaṇḍakī (Translated from Pali by Bhikkhu Sujato)*. (n.d.). SuttaCentral. Retrieved July 17, 2025, from https://suttacentral.net/an5.141/en/sujato
11. *AN 5.161: Aghatavinaya Sutta: Subduing Hatred (1) (Translated from Pali by Thanissaro Bhikkhu)*. (n.d.). Accesstoinsight.org. Retrieved July 17, 2025, from https://www.accesstoinsight.org/tipitaka/an/an05/an05.161.than.html
12. *AN 5.167: Codanāsutta: Resentment- Accusation (Translated from Pali by Bhikkhu Sujato)*. (n.d.). SuttaCentral. Retrieved July 17, 2025, from https://suttacentral.net/an5.167/en/sujato
13. *AN 5.204: Balasutta: With Kimbila - Powers (Translated from Pali by Bhikkhu Sujato)*. (n.d.). SuttaCentral. Retrieved July 17, 2025, from https://suttacentral.net/an5.204/en/sujato

14. *AN 7.7: Ugga sutta: To ugga (Translated from Pali by Thanissaro Bhikkhu)*. (n.d.). Accesstoinsight.org. Retrieved July 17, 2025, from https://www.accesstoinsight.org/tipitaka/an/an07/an07.007.than.html

15. *AN 7.35: Mitta sutta: A friend (Translated from Pali by Thanissaro Bhikkhu)*. (n.d.). Accesstoinsight.org. Retrieved July 17, 2025, from https://www.accesstoinsight.org/tipitaka/an/an07/an07.035.than.html

16. *AN 7.61: Pacalāyamānasutta: 6. The Undeclared Points Nodding Off (Translated from Pali by Bhikkhu Sujato)*. (n.d.). SuttaCentral. Retrieved July 8, 2025, from https://suttacentral.net/an7.61/en/sujato?lang=en&layout=plain&reference=none&notes=asterisk&highlight=false&script=latin

17. *AN 7.64: Kodhanasutta: 6. The Undeclared Points- Irritable (Translated froom Pali by Bhikkhu Sujato)*. (n.d.). SuttaCentral. Retrieved July 9, 2025, from https://suttacentral.net/an7.64/en/sujato?lang=en&layout=plain&reference=none&notes=asterisk&highlight=false&script=latin

18. *AN 8.54: Dīghajāṇusutta: With Dīghajāṇu (Translated from Pali by Bhikkhu Sujato)*. (n.d.). SuttaCentral. Retrieved July 18, 2025, from https://suttacentral.net/an8.54/en/sujato

19. *AN 10.54: Samatha sutta: With regard to tranquility (Translated from Pali by Thanissaro Bhikkhu)*. (n.d.). Accesstoinsight.org. Retrieved July 18, 2025, from https://www.accesstoinsight.org/tipitaka/an/an10/an10.054.than.html

20. *Dhammapada Verse 24: Kumbhaghosakasetthi Vatthu (Translated by Daw Mya Tin, M A)*. (n.d.). Tipitaka.net. Retrieved July 7, 2025, from https://www.tipitaka.net/tipitaka/dhp/verseload.php?verse=024

21. *Dhammapada Verse 50: Paveyya ajivaka Vatthu (Translated by Daw Mya Tin, M A)*. (n.d.). Tipitaka.net. Retrieved July 5, 2025, from https://www.tipitaka.net/tipitaka/dhp/verseload.php?verse=050

22. *Dhammapada Verse 67: Kassaka Vatthu (Translated by Daw Mya Tin, M A)*. (n.d.). Tipitaka.net. Retrieved July 7, 2025, from https://www.tipitaka.net/tipitaka/dhp/verseload.php?verse=067

23. *Dhammapada Verse 76 Radhatthera Vatthu (Translated by Daw Mya Tin, M A)*. (n.d.). Tipitaka.net. Retrieved July 18, 2025, from https://www.tipitaka.net/tipitaka/dhp/verseload.php?verse=076

24. *Dhammapada Verse 114: Kisagotami Vatthu (Translated by Daw Mya Tin, M A)*. (n.d.). Tipitaka.net. Retrieved July 7, 2025, from https://www.tipitaka.net/tipitaka/dhp/verseload.php?verse=114

25. *Dhammapada Verse 124: Kukkutamittanesada Vatthu (Translated by Daw Mya Tin, M A)*. (n.d.). Tipitaka.net. Retrieved July 7, 2025, from https://www.tipitaka.net/tipitaka/dhp/verseload.php?verse=124

26. *Dhammapada Verse 125: Kokasunakhaluddaka Vatthu (Translated by Daw Mya Tin, M A)*. (n.d.). Tipitaka.net. Retrieved July 9, 2025, from https://www.tipitaka.net/tipitaka/dhp/verseload.php?verse=125

27. *Dhammapada Verse 129: Chabbaggiya Bhikkhu Vatthu (Translated by Daw Mya Tin, M A)*. (n.d.). Tipitaka.net. Retrieved July 18, 2025, from https://www.tipitaka.net/tipitaka/dhp/verseload.php?verse=129

28. *Dhammapada Verse 133: Kondadhanatthera Vatthu (Translated by Daw Mya Tin, M A)*. (n.d.). Tipitaka.net. Retrieved July 18, 2025, from https://www.tipitaka.net/tipitaka/dhp/verseload.php?verse=133

29. *Dhammapada Verse 160: Kumarakassapamatuttheri Vatthu (Translated by Daw Mya Tin, M A).* (n.d.). Tipitaka.net. Retrieved July 9, 2025, from https://www.tipitaka.net/tipitaka/dhp/verseload.php?verse=160
30. *Dhammapada Verse 176: Cincamanavika Vatthu (Translated by Daw Mya Tin, M A).* (n.d.). Tipitaka.net. Retrieved July 9, 2025, from https://www.tipitaka.net/tipitaka/dhp/verseload.php?verse=176
31. *Dhammapada Verse 223: Uttara Upasika Vatthu (Translated by Daw Mya Tin, M A).* (n.d.). Tipitaka.net. Retrieved July 9, 2025, from https://www.tipitaka.net/tipitaka/dhp/verseload.php?verse=223
32. *Dhammapada Verse 227-230: Atula Upasaka Vatthu (Translated by Daw Mya Tin, M A).* (n.d.). Tipitaka.net. Retrieved July 11, 2025, from https://www.tipitaka.net/tipitaka/dhp/verseload.php?verse=227
33. *Dhammapada Verse 234: Chabbaggiya Vatthu (Translated by Daw Mya Tin, M A).* (n.d.). Tipitaka.net. Retrieved July 11, 2025, from https://www.tipitaka.net/tipitaka/dhp/verseload.php?verse=231
34. *Dhammapada Verse 252: Mendakasetthi Vatthu (Translated by Daw Mya Tin, M A).* (n.d.). Tipitaka.net. Retrieved July 11, 2025, from https://www.tipitaka.net/tipitaka/dhp/verseload.php?verse=252
35. *Dhammapada Verse 256: Vinicchayamahamatta Vatthu (Translated by Daw Mya Tin, M A).* (n.d.). Tipitaka.net. Retrieved July 11, 2025, from https://www.tipitaka.net/tipitaka/dhp/verseload.php?verse=256
36. *Dhammapada Verse 291: Kukkutandakhadika Vatthu (Translated by Daw Mya Tin, M A).* (n.d.). Tipitaka.net. Retrieved July 11, 2025, from https://www.tipitaka.net/tipitaka/dhp/verseload.php?verse=291
37. *Dhammapada Verse 304: Culasubhadda Vatthu (Translated by Daw Mya Tin, M A).* (n.d.). Tipitaka.net. Retrieved July 11, 2025, from https://www.tipitaka.net/tipitaka/dhp/verseload.php?verse=304
38. *Dhammapada Verse 327: Paveyyakahatthi Vatthu (Translated by Daw Mya Tin, M A).* (n.d.). Tipitaka.net. Retrieved July 12, 2025, from https://www.tipitaka.net/tipitaka/dhp/verseload.php?verse=327
39. *DN 22: Maha-satipatthana sutta: The great frames of reference (Translated from the Pali by Thanissaro Bhikkhu).* (n.d.). Accesstoinsight.org. Retrieved July 12, 2025, from https://www.accesstoinsight.org/tipitaka/dn/dn.22.0.than.html
40. *MN 9: Sammādiṭṭhisutta: Right View (Translated from Pali by Bhikkhu Sujato).* (n.d.). SuttaCentral. Retrieved July 18, 2025, from https://suttacentral.net/mn9/en/sujato
41. *MN 20: Vitakkasaṇṭhānasutta: How to Stop Thinking (Translated from Pali by Bhikkhu Sujato).* (n.d.). SuttaCentral. Retrieved July 17, 2025, from https://suttacentral.net/mn20/en/sujato
42. *MN 22: Alagaddūpamasutta: The Simile of the Cobra (Translated from Pali by Bhikkhu Sujato).* (n.d.). SuttaCentral. Retrieved July 17, 2025, from https://suttacentral.net/mn22/en/sujato
43. *MN 121: Cūḷasuññatasutta: The Shorter Discourse on Emptiness (Translated from Pali by Bhikkhu Sujato).* (n.d.). SuttaCentral. Retrieved July 16, 2025, from https://suttacentral.net/mn121/en/sujato?lang=en&layout=plain&reference=none&notes=asterisk&highlight=false&script=latin
44. *Pali Canon.* (n.d.). Everydayzen.org. Retrieved July 18, 2025, from https://everydayzen.org/studyguide/pali-canon/
45. *Sanghakaya Foundation.* (n.d.). Sanghakaya.org. Retrieved July 18, 2025, from https://sanghakaya.org/

46. *Sn 1.3: Khaggavisana sutta: A rhinoceros (Translated from Pali by Thanissaro Bhikkhu)*. (n.d.). Accesstoinsight.org. Retrieved July 17, 2025, from https://www.accesstoinsight.org/tipitaka/kn/snp/snp.1.03.than.html

47. *SN 35:101 Not Yours: Na Tumhāka Sutta (Translated from the Pali by Thanissaro Bhikkhu)*. (n.d.). Dhammatalks.org. Retrieved July 8, 2025, from https://www.dhammatalks.org/suttas/SN/SN35_101.html

48. *SN 45.1: Avijja sutta: Ignorance (translated from Pali by Thanissaro Bhikkhu)*. (n.d.). Accesstoinsight.org. Retrieved July 16, 2025, from https://www.accesstoinsight.org/tipitaka/sn/sn45/sn45.001.than.html

49. *SN 45.8: Magga-vibhanga sutta: An analysis of the path (translated from Pali by Thanissaro Bhikkhu)*. (n.d.). Accesstoinsight.org. Retrieved July 12, 2025, from https://www.accesstoinsight.org/tipitaka/sn/sn45/sn45.008.than.html

50. *Snp 1.8: Mettasutta: Loving-Kindness (Translated from Pali by Laurence Khantipalo Mills)*. (n.d.). SuttaCentral. Retrieved July 17, 2025, from https://suttacentral.net/snp1.8/en/mills

51. *Snp 4.15: Attadaṇḍasutta: Taking Up Arms (Translated from Pali by Bhikkhu Sujato). (n.d.). SuttaCentral. Retrieved July 18, 2025, from https://suttacentral.net/snp4.15/en/sujato*

52. *Tipitaka: The Pali Canon*. (n.d.). Accesstoinsight.org. Retrieved July 18, 2025, from https://www.accesstoinsight.org/tipitaka/

53. *Ud 1.10: Bāhiya Sutta: Bāhiya (Translated from Pali by Thanissaro Bhikkhu)*. (n.d.). Accesstoinsight.org. Retrieved July 18, 2025, from https://www.accesstoinsight.org/tipitaka/kn/ud/ud.1.10.than.html

54. *Zen koans*. (n.d.). Ashidakim.com. Retrieved July 18, 2025, from https://ashidakim.com/zenkoans

About the Author

Sati Siroda crafts narratives that transcend age, speaking to the universal human spirit. Drawing from a multifaceted background in engineering, research, education, business, and communication, Sati crafts stories that resonate across generations and speak to a deep, holistic understanding of the mind.

The Art of the Reflective Pattern

Sati's signature style is defined by *intentional simplicity*. She writes in clear, accessible English, placing profound weight on every word. Her work utilizes *gentle reflective patterns*—an intentional method aimed at mirroring how the human brain preserves wisdom over time. This guarantees her message of courage and self-discovery is not merely read but profoundly experienced—almost as if it were a manifestation that embeds itself in the reader's consciousness.

A Holistic Approach to Growth

Sati explores a vast range of genres, from fiction to insightful non-fiction. Regardless of the form her writing takes, an *"inspirational angle"* remains her north star, ensuring that every book serves as a catalyst for personal evolution. Her expertise extends into several key pillars:

- *Inspiration & Empowerment:* She is dedicated to creating "stepping stone" literary pieces that inspire courage, emotional intelligence, and the confidence to pursue dreams fearlessly.
- *Mindfulness & Meditation:* As a dedicated practitioner, Sati blends timeless wisdom with gentle insights, helping readers navigate the modern world with clarity, presence, and calm.
- *Healthy Living & Herbal Wisdom:* She integrates her holistic perspective into practical guides for healthy living, exploring the synergy between nature, nutrition, and mental well-being.

Sati leverages her diverse skills in teaching, research, entrepreneurship, and writing to craft intuitive stories that act as universal tools for resilience and self-love. Each word is carefully chosen to promote emotional growth, enabling readers of all ages and backgrounds to face life's difficulties with creativity, optimism, and purpose. Through her captivating books, Sati inspires everyone to pursue self-discovery, demonstrating that the right words, arranged in the right patterns, can unlock our inner potential.

www.ingramcontent.com/pod-product-compliance
Ingram Content Group UK Ltd.
Pitfield, Milton Keynes, MK11 3LW, UK
UKHW021406190726
13845UKWH00028B/908

9 788198 611703